1,000 Creative Writing Prompts, Volume 2: More Ideas for Blogs, Scripts, Stories and More

Bryan Cohen and
Jeremiah Jones

DEDICATION

I dedicate this book to my wife for keeping me focused and happy.

CONTENTS

INTRODUCTION

It was Christmas 2008 and I was working on a last ditch plan. I'd gotten myself into a mountain of debt due to a failed video project that I'd tried to fund on credit cards. It didn't work and I resorted to finding money any way I could, including staying in Chicago during a potential family vacation and instead answering phones at a marketing company located in a downtown skyscraper. Most of the company's employees were home for the holidays, giving me about seven hours of free time during the eight hour shift. For weeks, I'd been reading about a website creation program called Site Build It, but I'd been too scared to leap in. Partly out of boredom and partly out of a desperation approach to make a little extra money, I began my website Build Creative Writing Ideas (which can be found at http://www.build-creative-writing-ideas.com).

At first, the site was a general rehashing of every personal development trope I'd learned, applied to writing. There were a lot of motivation techniques and personal time management ideas, but there weren't that many pages dedicated solely to writing. After seeing that the term "creative writing prompts" had some strong Google traffic capabilities, I tried my hand at writing a page. I did a bit of research and found that most writing prompts were both short and blasé. They didn't strike at the heart, they didn't really make you think and they didn't mine the depths of the imagination. I wasn't all that confident in my writing by that point, but I had a feeling that I could make these prompts mean something to the people reading and using them. I had a natural ability to come up with ideas in general, due to my improv comedy background, which had required me to come up with dozens of ideas during each practice or show. After creating a few of these pages, I noticed that they pulled in much more traffic than my motivational pages ever had. I continued to write as many prompts as I could think up and my traffic continued to grow.

Around a year into the life of my site, I began to hear about the wonderfulness that is self-publishing, though I didn't yet know that authors could do it through the major online retailers like Amazon and Barnes & Noble. I was still struggling with money and while people were coming to my site, I wasn't really converting much of the traffic into cold, hard cash. I thought a book couldn't hurt, and I looked to the prompts for guidance. I had around 700 prompts written at the time. If I kept writing until I hit 1,000, I thought that perhaps it'd be a substantial enough book that people would be willing to buy it. I pushed myself to finish the final 300 prompts and put the book out in PDF form. It had some issues with formatting and editing and for a while, my future wife's mother was the only one who had purchased it, but somehow I learned that Amazon had opened a self-publishing platform. I released the book there, sent it along to a few bloggers for reviews and hoped for the best.

Selling my first copy to a complete stranger on Amazon was amazing. I felt like a legitimate author for the first time in my life. When it sold an average of one book per day in its second month, I knew that it wasn't much money to go on but it was a fantastic start. By Christmas 2010, the book sold over 100 copies in a single month. It continued to grow for several consecutive months and I tried a blog tour to spread the word about the book, the website and the rest of my work. The tour pushed my sales higher than they'd ever been at an average of 25 books per day. I started to pay down some of my debt and write other books about writing, but none had the selling power of the original *1,000 Creative Writing Prompts* book. The book literally changed my life and my career. Before I released it, I was a struggling temp hoping to be a writer and a performer someday. Now, after selling more than 20,000 copies, I'm finally coming into my own as a creative person. I know that my prompts can make a difference in the writing world.

Enough About Me

Perhaps I've talked a bit too much about myself here. Let's talk about the prompts. What makes these creative writing prompts different from others? At first, my thought was that I tried harder than the other prompt writers. In reality, the difference has to do with how the brain works. I end nearly 90 percent of my prompts with a question. The human brain absolutely loves questions. If you ask your brain a question it wants to figure out the answer at all costs. If you ask your brain a question that relates to your imagination, such as why a character acts in a certain way or what will happen next in a wild scenario, the creative parts of your brain get extremely excited and begin shooting answers at you almost immediately. And isn't that the point of a prompt; to get your creative juices flowing so that you can put words down on the page without thinking too much?

Do I have any evidence to back up these claims? Sure! I've had some awesome responses to the prompts and the book. I've had people tell me that they've used the prompts to write essays and assignments. I've seen bloggers take my prompts and use them to create blog posts and stories. I've even had several people inform me that the prompts have helped them while writing a novel, with one author telling me that a prompt I wrote helped them to create a novel *from scratch*. Imagine that. What if a book of 1,000 prompts could have 1,000 novels worth of inspiration within its pages? That's what I'm hoping for and that's one of the reasons I'm writing a sequel.

The first set of 1,000 creative writing prompts was pretty much whatever I could think of on a given day to put down on paper. It was raw and fun and I didn't really know what I was doing. A couple years later with more knowledge of how prompts work and how people use them has been a major help in writing a new 1,000. I can cover different subjects and can use the maturity gathered from a couple of extra years. I can also make more of the prompts family friendly after realizing that many parents have bought the first book to use with their kids. This will give me the ability to later adapt the book into workbooks and a journal as I did with my first couple of prompt books.

How and When to Use the Prompts

As I mentioned before, I've had people tell me about using the prompts for schoolwork and novels, but that's not all. I've seen writers use the prompts for poetry and songwriting, journal writing and blogging and even as conversation starters at a party. You can use the prompts to help you get a boost if you have no ideas at all, or they can help you to move ahead if you've got an idea that's stuck in the mud. Simply scroll down to one of the prompts in this book. You can read it aloud, read it silently or even re-write it word-for-word or with a slight adaptation. Let the prompt sink into your head for a second or two and then write. With writing prompts, I think the best policy is to write as quickly as you can without thinking. You can always go back to your work later and edit out any spelling or grammatical errors. Now is not the time for perfection. Plenty of writers write inspired but flawed first drafts. They all have one thing in common though. They actually finish those first drafts. Utilize these prompts to get that first draft on paper. Once you've gotten that far, then you can re-write to your heart's content and self-publish or find a publisher at your leisure.

I'm a big proponent of writing in the morning, as early in the morning as you can stand it. If you've read some of my other work, you'll know that I'm not a big fan of coffee, as I believe it messes with the mind's ability to be creative more than a few hours straight. If I were you, I'd practice getting up early, sans-stimulation, and get to your writing desk or area as quickly as possible. Don't dally too long or you'll miss out on the little amount of time you might have available for writing. If the morning isn't the best time for you, feel free to pick another time, it's just important to make that writing time consistent. Not three days a week or every Saturday, I mean every single day. When I began writing this book, I was in the midst of a 365-day-straight, 2,500-word per day challenge. I'll admit that this challenge was difficult on some occasions, but by forcing my hand to write every day without a break, I was able to create so much more than I would have if left to my own devices. During the challenge, I finished multiple books, which can be found wherever fine e-books are sold.

You don't have to write 2,500 words a day or even set a word count goal at all. I do think you should create at least one goal for yourself, though, because it will ensure that you write each day without skipping it. Perhaps the first goal can be to write at least five minutes a day. Everyone should be able to fit in at least five minutes somewhere! Once you've done a whole month of five minutes per day, try to up your tolerance to 10 minutes or 20. Try adding in a word count goal or a chapter goal. There are so many different writing goals and challenges you can give yourself and I suggest that you take as many on as you can with the aid of this book.

Viva La Creativity!

I believe that the way our school system is working, creativity is weeded out earlier and earlier. In some school districts, such important classes as art, music and drama are being cut due to funding problems. In the past, these classes helped to reveal to students that they could be artistic and creative. In more academic classrooms, such as English and writing, test scores have become more important than creative writing allowing schools can get more funding and can reach certain ridiculous quotas. This is a creativity epidemic and it needs to stop somewhere.

If you're one of the victims of a lack of creative exposure growing up or you have children who are dealing with the same issues, it's time to fight back. Use these prompts to create! Write stories, even if they're bad, so that you can creatively express yourself. Creativity is a wonderful human ability and it should never be suppressed! I hope that you use and share this book with as many people as possible who have the like-minded desires to stay imaginative throughout their lives and to mine every single day for their inherited creative abilities. Happy writing!

Sincerely,
Bryan Cohen, Co-Author of *1,000 Creative Writing Prompts, Volume 2: More Ideas for Blogs, Scripts and Stories and More*

CHAPTER 1: TIME AND PLACE

The Past

1. If you could travel back to any time in the past, what date would you choose and why? Would you attempt to influence past events while you were there? Why or why not?

2. What past memory do you cherish the most and why? If you could trade that memory for something amazing to happen in the future, would you do it? Why or why not?

3. What past decade or century would you consider your favorite and why? Do you think you'd be happier living back then or in the present day and why?

4. What is your biggest regret from the past and why? What did you learn from this incident and how has it helped you going forward?

5. A time traveler from the future says that he needs your help to right some wrongs in the past. Do you trust this stranger and help him on his mission? Why or why not? After your decision, what happens next?

6. Why do you think some people only focus on their "glory days," their great successes from the past? How might you keep yourself from looking entirely backwards in the future?

7. After nearly a decade of no contact, an important person from your past has come back into your life. What questions do you have for them? Would you welcome this person with open arms? Why or why not?

8. If you could send yourself a message several years in the past, what would it be and why? How might getting message in the past change you in the present?

9. What is the most important lesson you've learned from studying your own past experiences? Would you consider teaching that lesson to others? Why or why not?

10. It's been said that the negative events of the past will repeat themselves if we fail to learn from our mistakes. Do you agree with that statement? Why or why not? How might the statement apply in your life?

The Present

11. What is one trait you have today that you might not have in the future? Do you think that change will be for better or for worse and why?

12. What are three things that distinguish the present day from the past and future? How may people look at those aspects of today differently 20 years from now?

13. It's been said that to be happy, you have to live in the moment. Do you agree with that statement? Why or why not? How well do you think you live in the moment and why do you believe that?

14. A mystical watchmaker has given you an opportunity to change a key aspect of present-day society. What part of the present would you change and why? How would this change affect your daily routine?

15. What are the top three things you think need to change about the way the world is today? What role will you play in changing them and why?

16. People like to talk about the past and plan for the future. What recommendations would you have for someone who wants to live in the now? How would those suggestions impact that person's life?

17. Think back to a time that you really seized the moment in a given situation. How did your actions make you feel? What would your life be like if you lived like that all of the time and why?

18. What is something the past did better than the present day? Do you think that regression will improve going forward or get worse and why?

19. What are some parts of the present that will be completely gone in the future? Will you miss them when they're gone? Why or why not?

20. When historians talk about the present day, what nickname do you think they'd give it and why? Would that nickname effectively convey the world you lived in? Why or why not?

The Future

21. What are you most looking forward to in the immediate future and why? What are you looking forward to in the next couple of years and why?

22. In 10 years, how will your life be different? Will it be better, worse, or the same, and why?

23. One hundred years ago, authors and other storytellers thought we'd have flying cars and apartments on Mars by now. How do you think the world will look 100 years from now? How long might it take for the future to really look like "the future" and why?

24. As the world changes, some technologies and jobs will become irrelevant. What careers might be obsolete in the future? What jobs might spring up to replace them?

25. You've inherited the ability to dream about the future. How will you use this new gift? Do you think it'll change your actions? Why or why not?

26. What do you think will be the next big invention or the wave of the future? How would your life change if you were the one to create such a thing?

27. What will have to change in the world to make sure the future is a better place for the next few generations? How can you contribute to that change?

28. Do you think the future will bring positive changes, negative changes, or a mix of both? What is some evidence to support your answer?

29. Do you think fortunetellers actually have the ability to tell the future? Why or why not?

30. What are the top five things you want to change for you in the future? How likely do you think they are to happen and why?

The Future #2

31. You look into a crystal ball and see far into the distant future. How does the world look? What has changed?

32. A supernatural being comes to you and says that he will give you the ability to design your ideal future. What world do you create and why?

33. Describe an event in your near future that you are looking forward to. What about this event is so special to you?

34. A mad scientist sends you into the future! What year does he send you to? What do you have to do in order to return to your own time?

35. If you saw far into your own future, how would it change the way you live your life and why? How would your knowledge affect the people around you?

36. In order to create a better future, we need to learn from the past. What lessons from your past will help you in the future? And why are these lessons so important?

37. The world has descended into chaos! How has this come about? How do you survive in this dystopian future?

38. A voodoo shaman approaches you with a proposition. You can either roll a pair of dice to potentially earn an amazing future or you can let your life play out as it would have if you had never met him. What do you decide to do and why? What happens next?

39. If you always knew what was going to happen in the next hour, how would it inform your choices and why?

40. One million years into the future, the world has been taken over by

another species from our planet. What species evolves to dominate humans? How do your descendants fit into this new world order?

The Morning

41. Describe your perfect morning. What would you do, who would you be with and how would you feel at the end of it all?

42. When you have a free morning, how do you take advantage of this time? How does this kind of morning differ from a morning filled with important things to do and why?

43. Are you a morning person? Why do you think some people are morning people? Besides getting up early, how do morning people differ from afternoon/evening/late night people?

44. What do you normally eat for breakfast? Why is this your go-to meal in the morning?

45. What activity would you consider to be an absolute necessity in the morning? Why is it so important? If you skipped this, would the rest of your day be shot? Why or why not?

46. How do you usually feel the moment you wake up? Do you think this feeling will change over time or be the same forever and why?

47. You're stuck in a time warp, forced to live the same morning over and over again! What would you do to keep things interesting during your predicament? Would this situation be more hellish or heavenly, and why?

48. Your chipper friend has gotten you up early enough to watch the sunrise. How does seeing this phenomenon make you feel and why? Is it something you'd do again? Why or why not?

49. What is the importance of having a morning routine? Are your mornings usually identical from day to day or do they change? Is one way better than the other? Why or why not?

50. What are some activities you can do in the morning that you couldn't do later on? How often do you do these and why?

The Afternoon

51. The best part of the afternoon is often lunchtime. What are your top three lunches and why? Is there anyway you could make them even better? Why or why not?

52. How do you feel at work or school when 2:30 p.m. rolls around? How might you be able to feel differently at that time?

53. What's something you love doing during the afternoon that you don't get to do on a regular basis? How would you feel if you could do it every single day of your life and why?

54. Afternoons can vary a lot from season to season. If you could pick a

free afternoon to do as you pleased in any season, which one would it be and why?

55. Would you rather spend a Sunday afternoon being lazy, partying, or getting work done and why? How would your life change if you spent every afternoon that way and why?

56. During the warmer months, the afternoon can be the hottest time of the day. Would you rather be outside or inside during those hot and sunny hours and why? What if you had to do work while you were outside?

57. Describe how one afternoon might be different with these different sets of people: your parents, your friends, your siblings, and a group of five-year-olds you have to babysit.

58. If you've ever had a sick day at home, you know that afternoon TV isn't always the best. Imagine you're the head of a major TV network and you want to revolutionize daytime TV. How do you do it? Are you successful? Why or why not?

59. Think back to the best afternoon you've ever had. Why was it so awesome? What would you have to do to repeat or top such a memorable day?

60. You and your family have moved to a place in the world with very little sunlight. How will your afternoons change when they're completely shrouded in darkness? What will you miss the most about those sunny days and why?

The Evening

61. What is your favorite thing to do in the evening when all of your work/homework/chores are done? Would you do something different if you had no work to do? Why or why not?

62. Evenings can get packed pretty easily with work, practices, social activities, and more. Do you think your evenings are too busy? Why or why not? Is there a middle ground between overworked and bored? If so, what is it?

63. We've come a long way since microwave TV dinners in the 1950s. What is the most gourmet dinner you've ever had? Do you think it was too fancy? Why or why not?

64. If you could watch a sunset from anywhere in the world, where would you choose and why? Who would you watch it with, if you had the choice?

65. Imagine you came from a very strict family that always made you go to bed before 7 p.m. What would you miss the most in those last few hours of evening and why?

66. A massive storm has blown out the power to all TV stations and the internet for an entire week! How will you spend your evenings differently

and why?

67. How might your evening routine change given the following situations: living alone, married, raising twin infants, and during vacation?

68. How would you life change if every evening you had to go to a different party? Would you get partied out? Why or why not?

69. Some people like actors, restaurant servers, and customer service representatives have to work almost every evening. What would it be like if you never had your evenings free? How would your mornings and afternoons change and why?

70. If you could live a week's worth of evenings at any age (past, present, or future) what age would you choose and why? How can you bring the best parts of those evenings into your current routine?

Weekend

71. Who are the top five people you'd like to spend time with on the weekend and why? How often do you actually get to hang out with them and what activities do you participate in when you do?

72. You are spending the weekend driving out of town to hang out with extended family. Is this positive or negative and why? What will you do when you get there?

73. Describe your ideal Sunday morning. When would you get up, what would you do, and how would you feel while doing it?

74. What are some of the things you have to do on the weekend? How much do they cut into your attempt to have an awesome weekend?

75. A well-timed snowstorm has given you a four-day weekend! What will you do with these extra two days? How does a weather-caused extended weekend differ from a planned four-day holiday?

76. Would you rather spend your weekends in or out on the town and why? What are your favorite activities in either environment and why?

77. Your family is giving you a choice for your next weekend getaway! What place do you choose and why? Would it be fun for everyone involved? Why or why not?

78. What was your favorite weekend that you can remember? What caused this weekend to stick out in your mind? What would you have to do to top it and why?

79. Which of the following weekend activities would be your top choice and why: Sunday brunch, opening night at the movie theater, a friend's birthday party or bowling night out with the family? Which would be your bottom choice? Why?

80. How would your life be different if there were five days off work and school and only two days with set obligations? Would this be a better or worse world to live in and why?

The 1960s

81. In what ways would a civil rights rally in the 1960s be different from one today? If you had been your current age back then, would you attend such a rally? Why or why not?

82. You have been drafted to go into the Vietnam War. How do you react to this news? Will you report to your new post or try to flee the country and why?

83. In what ways would your life be different if you were born in the 1960s? Do you think your life would be better, worse, or about the same and why?

84. You have traded places with Neil Armstrong for his 1969 trip to the moon! Describe your first steps on the moon's surface. Would you change Armstrong's historic line to make it your own? Why or why not?

85. The 1960s saw the birth of some iconic bands like The Beatles and The Rolling Stones. Which band from the 1960s would you most like to see live in its heyday and why? How would such a concert differ from one held today and why?

86. When President John F. Kennedy was shot and killed in 1963, it was a moment many people at the time would remember for their whole lives. What would a parallel moment be from your life and why? Where were you when it happened and how did you react?

87. Like any decade, the 1960s had its own style and language. How would your friends react if you started dressing and talking like you were from the 60s? Would any of them mimic you and join along? Why or why not?

88. If you could meet one famous figure from the 1960s, who would it be and why? What kind of advice might this person have for your life? How would you follow it?

89. While browsing at a vintage clothing shop, you've been transported back in time to live a day in the 1960s! What wouldn't you be able to do back then that you could do today? How would you try to blend in? Would you enjoy your experience? Why or why not?

90. If you lived in the 1960s, would you be more likely to be a part of the counterculture or the mainstream and why? How would your family feel about your choice and why?

The 1970s

91. In 1977, the movie Star Wars became a massive success and made the Science Fiction genre a mainstream hit. What would it have been like to be in line for Star Wars on opening day? Who would you have gone with and how would you all have reacted to the new and extremely popular

picture?

92. At the time, the 1970s was referred to as the Me Generation. Do you think people are more self-absorbed now then they were back then and why might that be the case?

93. You and your friends have been sent back in time to a Disco club in the 1970s! Describe what outfits you'd have to wear to fit in. How would your dance moves compare to the moves of the regulars?

94. Video and computer games came about in the 1970s, though they look nothing like the cinematic games of today. How would a person from the 1970s react to games like Halo III? Would it ruin games from the 70s for this person? Why or why not?

95. It wasn't until 1971 that people between the ages of 18 and 21 could vote. Do you think the current voting age of 18 is fair? Why or why not?

96. President Richard Nixon was the only President to ever resign from office in 1974 after he was implicated in the Watergate Scandal. How might you have felt back then if you'd voted for Nixon? Do you think a similar incident could happen in this day and age? Why or why not?

97. Today's world is very interdependent, given the internet and social networking. How would the world change if technology reverted back to how it was in the 1970s? How would your life change, given that personal computers cost around $5,000 at the time?

98. During the oil crisis in 1973 and 1974, 20 percent of gas stations had no fuel at all to provide consumers. How would your day-to-day life be different if you and your family simply couldn't get gas? What changes might you have to make during such a crisis and why?

99. In 1979, the world officially eradicated smallpox, a deadly disease. Imagine that you've created a vaccine for a terrible disease that could save millions of lives. How would you get it to as many people as possible? Would you try to get a lot of money for your invention? Why or why not?

100. If you were sent back to the 1970s, what would you miss the most about living in the present day and why? Would there be aspects of today you'd be happy to be rid of? Why or why not?

The 1980s

101. The 1980s brought the invention of the internet. What do you think it would have been like to be one of the web's first users? In what ways might it have been different from the internet today?

102. On December 8, 1980, former member of The Beatles John Lennon was shot dead. What would it be like if one of your favorite musicians from today was murdered? How would you react and what would you do to grieve?

103. The movie The Empire Strikes Back, famous for Darth Vader's

reveal to Luke Skywalker, entered theaters in 1980. How would you have reacted if you saw the movie on opening night, completely spoiler-free? How would audiences today receive such a plot twist?

104. MTV captivated the world when it launched with a collection of music videos in 1981. What do you think will be the next big thing in music? Do you think this development will be positive or negative and why?

105. The highest grossing film of the 1980s was E.T. The Extra-Terrestrial, which was released in 1982. What would you do if you came upon a small, friendly alien in your house? Would you protect it from the government like in the movie or keep out of trouble? Why would you choose that route?

106. The World Wrestling Federation (now World Wrestling Entertainment) became huge in the 1980s on the back of stars like Hulk Hogan and Macho Man Randy Savage. What would your day-to-day life be like if you were a popular 80s wrestler? Would the fame be worth all the bumps and bruises on the mat?

107. Athletes Magic Johnson and Larry Bird faced off against each other in three National Basketball Association finals in the 1980s. Do you think competitors need a rival to reach their best performance? Why or why not?

108. Boycotts took place at both the 1980 and 1984 Olympics because of political issues between the Western world and communist countries. How would you feel if politics got in the way of your ability to play sports or participate in any other activity? Would you try to get around the boycott? Why or why not?

109. The popularity of the Nintendo Entertainment System in the mid to late 80s gave the period the nickname "The Nintendo Era." Do you think the advent of popular video games was positive or negative for society and why? How would you have felt if you were the first person to get a Nintendo on your block and why?

110. The musician Madonna inspired multiple fashion trends from her music videos in the 80s. If you could inspire a new fashion trend, what would it be and why? How would you make sure the trend caught on?

The 1990s

111. Instant messaging on America Online (AOL) in the 1990s changed the way we communicate forever. Do you feel that change was for the better or worse and why? How important do you think writing letters and talking on the phone are in the present day?

112. In 1992, Hurricane Andrew devastated the south of Florida. How would you have coped with living through such a storm before widespread cell phone use and digital communication? How might such a massive

storm be different today?

113. The television show "Friends" debuted in 1994 and become a cultural phenomenon for over a decade. What would it be like to play the same character for 10+ years? Do you think you'd get bored? Why or why not?

114. The 1990s saw the spread of the grunge style. How would your family react if you came in sporting unwashed hair with a thrift shop flannel shirt? What might they want you to wear instead and why?

115. As the 1990s drew to a close, many people feared that computers would shut down as soon as the clocks rolled over to the year 2000. How would your life change if all computers shut down today? What would you miss the most about your computer-filled life and why?

116. E-commerce websites like Amazon.com became very popular in the 1990s. In what ways did this development help and hurt regular stores? Would you rather run a store online or in person and why?

117. Michael Jordan became a sports and pop culture icon in the 1990s when his Chicago Bulls won six National Basketball Association championships. If you could be the best at something in the entire world, what would you choose and why? What would be the pitfalls of being so famous?

118. After its release in 1998, the movie Titanic made close to $2 billion dollars worldwide. Why do you think this portrayal of the famous disaster was so popular around the world? What is another famous event in history that could make an amazing movie experience and why would people enjoy watching it?

119. The Gulf War started on August 2, 1990, when Saddam Hussein's Iraqi regime invaded and conquered Kuwait. In retaliation. the United Nations and the U.S. invaded to cut Iraq off from much of the world for over a decade. How would your life be different if your country was cut off from all other countries? How might you feel about the governments and people throughout the world?

120. Mother Theresa, a nun and a Nobel Peace Prize winner, died in 1997 after a life dedicated to service. Would you ever consider helping people as a full time profession without expecting much in return? Why or why not? How might you feel differently from people with regular jobs?

The 2000s

121. The launch of Facebook in the mid-2000s made social networking a worldwide craze. How would the world be different if Facebook was never created and why? Which would be better: a world with Facebook or a world without Facebook?

122. The late 2000s saw a global economic crisis. Do you feel like you

were impacted by the crisis? Why or why not? How might you stop another crisis from happening in the future?

123. How do you think the attacks of September 11, 2001, changed America forever? Do you think such an attack will happen again? Why or why not?

124. The World Meteorological Organization said in 2009 that the 2000s may have been the warmest decade since records began in 1850, adding fuel to the fire of global warming claims. Do you believe in global warming? Why or why not? What should the world do to reduce pollution and why?

125. In the 1990s, Peter Jackson directed the Lord of the Rings trilogy, bringing the classic J.R.R. Tolkien books to the screen. What classic work would you like to see turned into a movie? Who would you want to direct the film and why?

126. Reality TV dominated in the 2000s with shows like Survivor and The Hills. Do you think you'd ever want to be on a reality show? If so, which show would you pick and why? If not, why do you think reality shows are so popular?

127. The Harry Potter books became extremely popular during the 2000s, with the series selling more than 450 million copies in total. What is your idea for the next big young adult book series? Would it be as popular as Harry Potter? Why or why not?

128. Who would you say is the most influential celebrity of the 2000s? What would you do if you could trade places with him or her for a day? Would the experience make you more jealous, or would you be happier for your relatively anonymous life? Why?

129. In 2004, a massive earthquake and tsunami killed more than 200,000 people in 14 different countries. Why do you think an event like this isn't talked about nearly as much as 9/11, where the loss of life was much smaller? How would you try to help if you heard about such a terrible incident halfway across the globe and why?

130. In 2001, Grand Theft Auto III became one of the first immersive 3D gaming experiences. If you could create such a massive gaming experience, what would it be called and what would your character have to do during the game? How would it be similar and different to GTA III?

New York City

131. What is the first thing that comes to mind when you think of New York City? Do you think a New Yorker would appreciate the first thing that came to your mind? Why or why not?

132. New York City has a lot of history, culture and people, but what do you think is the most amazing thing about the city? Why do you think that ranks on top?

133. If you could produce any show on Broadway, what would it be and why? Would this play be worthy of the Broadway stage? Why or why not?

134. You are an immigrant in the early 1800s trying to get into the United States. How does seeing the Statue of Liberty for the first time make you feel and why?

135. How would you describe a typical New Yorker? Would you think the description was accurate if you were a New Yorker? Why or why not?

136. The United Nations, an international community of representatives from hundreds of countries around the world, holds its meetings in New York City. Do you think this is the best location for the U.N.? Why or why not?

137. When most people think of New York, they think of New York City. How do you picture the rest of the state of New York? Do you think New Yorkers who don't live in the city feel ignored? Why or why not?

138. After turning down an alley in New York City, you meet a man with a time machine. You can travel to any time period, but only within the city limits. What time period do you choose and why? Would you stay there to live out your days or come home and why?

139. Describe your ideal trip to New York City. What sights would you see and why? If you've been to the city, feel free to incorporate your experiences.

140. The rent in New York City makes it very difficult for a person making average wages to live there. Do you think it's worth the money? Why or why not? Could you survive a year paying top dollar for a tiny space? Why or why not?

U.S.A.

141. Where would you rank the U.S. in terms of greatness when compared to the other nations of the world? What does it mean to be a "great" country?

142. How do people from outside the U.S. typically view America and its citizens? Where do they get such a perspective? Is it accurate? Why or why not?

143. You've accepted the nomination to run for President of the United States! What are some of the features of your political platform? How will you convince your fellow Americans to vote for you?

144. What do you think it means to be an American? How has this definition changed from 50 years ago? How might it change in another 50 years?

145. Does being a U.S. citizen provide any advantages compared to citizens of other countries? Why or why not? What are some disadvantages?

146. The U.S. has come under fire for valuing safety and security above

privacy. Do you think it's worth tapping into phone and online records to prevent a few potential incidents of terrorism? Why or why not?

147. If you could add another state to the union, what place in the world would you want to add and why? Would you consider living there? Why or why not?

148. You've been transported back in time to the drafting of the U.S. Constitution. What advice would you have to give the drafters? Would they listen to you? Why or why not?

149. The U.S. has split in two and sunk into the Atlantic and Pacific Oceans! If you lived in the U.S., where would you and your family move and why? If not, what would the world's reaction be to the loss of the U.S. and why?

150. The U.S. has been called "the land of opportunity." Does that nickname still ring true? Why or why not?

Urban Life

151. What are some of the qualities that a child could develop growing up in the city versus growing up in the suburbs? Write a small story about the same kid growing up in both sets of circumstances and how different life would be for him or her in either one.

152. One of the major parts of urban life is dealing with congested streets and crowded train and bus platforms. Write a story focusing on a character trying to get from point A to point B in the city, with nothing "going his or her way." What are the obstacles and is the destination eventually met?

153. You knew you stayed out too late and now two shadowy figures appear to be following you. You pick up your pace and don't see a cab in sight. As the two individuals tap you on the shoulder, you hope for the best. What happens next?

154. As you crawl into bed in your tiny studio apartment, you wonder if city life is for you. While the offer is open to move back home and save more than $1,000 you currently pay per month for rent, you don't want to go backward in life. Your hand is forced when you lose your job abruptly. What do you decide to do and why?

155. You are getting ready to help your friend move. You don't blame him for asking; you couldn't afford movers either. What you do blame him for is living on the 6th floor with no elevator. Describe the pain-in-the-neck move from beginning to end. How do you and the other unpaid manual laborers cope?

156. When you think back to your hometown, you imagine the smell of lilac and honeysuckle plants. It helps you to get over your current smells of garbage, urine, and sewage that lurk around many city street corners. How

do you best deal with these prevalent urban odors and what other hygiene problems have you experienced city-side?

157. Many people looking to be in the entertainment industry flock to urban areas, which means you almost always have a friend in some kind of show. Write about a few of your uber-talented city friends and which of them has the best chance of making it. Why does this friend in particular have such star power?

158. Philly has cheese steaks, Chicago has deep dish, and New York has thin crust. Which city do you think has the best signature food style and why? Which one would you be the most likely to eat on a regular basis?

159. At first, the tourist attractions in your city were exciting, but you're realizing that they're too mainstream and overrun by tourists. What are some of the underground cool spots to see in your city that most people don't know about? Describe one such visit from beginning to end, detailing why this location deserves to stay completely secret.

160. Sports fans love their big city ability to visit a professional sports stadium as often as they like. Create a story in which you attend three major city sporting events in a single day. What do you eat and drink, who do you watch and what craziness do you experience in each separate venue? Do you think this city is the best in the world for the fans? Why or why not?

Suburban Life

161. What are the top five benefits of living in a suburb? What are the top five drawbacks of living in such an area? Write a story in which your main character experiences a few of each over the course of one day living in the sequestered middle-class burbs.

162. Some refer to the suburbs as an absence of real fun while others praise it for the security needed to raise a family. What is your reason for living the suburban life and would you pick it again if given a choice? Did all of the hopes you or your family had for the suburbs come true?

163. What are the most lively and happening late night spots in your suburban paradise? If you could create a secret bar or event venue to provide more youthful partying, what kind of place would it be and what would you and your friends do there?

164. What do you picture when you think of a typical suburban property? Describe the expertly painted exterior, the thoroughly manicured lawns, the ornamental decorations and the basketball hoop in the driveway. Do you think that most suburban properties meet this intricate standard? Why or why not?

165. You and your family have moved from the big city into the suburbs and your mom was quickly welcomed by the seemingly perfect women that appear to run this town. They fit the definition of the suburban housewife

so exactly that it's almost alien. Are these moms too good to be true and will your mother become one of them? What happens next?

166. It's a Friday night during your senior year of high school and your social options are limited. There are the typical chain restaurants like TGIFridays, the high school football game, or the lame house party. Describe your ho-hum social evening from beginning to end and include a dialogue with friends about what you'll do when you get out of this place.

167. Suburban television shows often demonstrate men as trying to hold onto their masculinity tooth and nail, but in reality, many feel as though they've already lost the battle. Dance recitals have replaced football Sundays and you can't even remember the last keg stand you did. Brainstorm a list and a plan of ways to get your man card back. Are any of them successful? Why or why not?

168. You and your spouse married, had kids, and went into a suburban life comparatively young. Now you're at the ripe old age of 50 and the kids are away at college or beyond. While most of your friends live in the area, you're hankering for a new adventure. What's the next step and why?

169. We've all seen them: the suburban neighborhood decoration battles around holiday time. Create a story in which two rival families battle for the top prize. What will the drama be before, during, and after the winner is selected and placed on the front page of the local paper?

170. It's one of the hottest days of the summer and the air conditioning is kaput. While you wait for the repairs, where do you take your kids to beat the heat within a five-mile radius? Can everyone agree on one destination or are you destined to have to break up hair-pulling and name-calling and why?

Restaurants

171. You have been given the choice to attend any restaurant in the world for your next birthday with all expenses paid. Describe how you go about making your decision. Which restaurant do you choose and why? Is your dining choice as exciting as you'd hoped?

172. Food television shows have made a major impact on independent restaurants. Whether the dining establishment has a ridiculous eating challenge or it got a 24-hour facelift, these food depositories benefit greatly from the publicity. If you could create your own restaurant show, what would be the focus and why? What restaurant would you feature on your program first?

173. Another major change to the dining industry has been the influx of daily deals from companies such as Groupon or Restaurant.com. How do you feel these new coupon sites have changes restaurants? Has it been for the better or the worse and why?

174. You and your friends have finally done it: you've leased out a

building for your very own restaurant! What kind of place is it, what's on your menu, which friends are helping you and why? What is your restaurant's name and how successful is it?

175. What is the restaurant that you went to the most as a kid with your family? Describe the decor, the food and the typical experience. What did you all usually order and did you tend to have a good time? Why or why not?

176. One of the ways that restaurant stay in business is by presenting an interesting or off-the-wall theme, such as peanut butter inspired menu items or a conveyer belt of sushi. What are some of the most interesting theme restaurants you've been to? How do you think you could have improved upon these theme ideas yourself?

177. You and your friends have just indulged in a greasy, disgusting meal at a hole in the wall burger joint you attend frequently. Suddenly, one of your friends becomes violently ill. Then another does. Soon after, all of you aren't feeling that hot. What happens next and will you ever trust that place again?

178. Restaurants can also be used for romance. Describe an experience, real or made up, in which you and a significant other had a fantastically romantic evening together. What did you wear, eat and talk about during this low-lit occasion?

179. Not everybody has had an opportunity to work in the wild world of food service, but imagine that you had to be a waiter or waitress during one of the busiest nights of the year. Write about your experience. How will you handle low tips and unruly customers? Does this evening change your perception of the restaurant business in general?

180. Some restaurants are directly connected with art. This can be in the form of a band or a solo violinist, a show or murder mystery, and even a live painter. How well do you think art and food mix? What would your ideal artistic experience be at a food establishment?

Amusement Parks

181. You and your friends have won a contest that gives your group sole access to your favorite amusement park without any strangers for an entire day. Without any lines and with nobody to slow you down, how do you best use your amusing day? What rides to you ride, what do you eat and what shows do you take in?

182. What is the scariest ride you've ever been on and why was it so scary? What was the lamest one? Describe your experiences with both, including how you felt before, during, and after.

183. Imagine that your design firm has been selected to create the most entertaining roller coaster imaginable. Describe the ride you create from

start to finish. What are the responses like for your company's brainchild?

184. One of the scariest experiences at a large public event like an amusement park is to get separated from your parents at a young age. Create a story from the perspective of the lost child. What happens and does everything get resolved in the end?

185. Amusement park food is like a collection of the worst offenders in heart disease and cavities rolled into one. What are some of your most memorable carnival meal choices and how did you feel after eating them? How would you feel right now if you wolfed down the exact same food combos in the comfort of your own home?

186. You are on a mission to defeat every rigged carnival game in the park. You have brought the equipment and months worth of planning necessary to obtain the largest stuffed animal possible at every single booth. Describe your scheme from beginning to end. Are you successful in your quest?

187. Imagine that you had one of the toughest jobs imaginable at a major theme park: you have to wear the giant mascot costume! What are your daily responsibilities as a giant animal or inanimate object? How do you survive the raucous kids and extreme temperatures?

188. After planning for months to have a giant birthday party at the local theme park, you finally get there, only to have a thunderstorm erupt! Most of the rides and attractions are closed. How do you attempt to salvage your waterlogged festivities?

189. Depending on the theme park you attend, you may be able to see an exciting stunt show. What do you think it's like to train for such a seemingly dangerous performance? Imagine that you were the star of the show. What would you feel like as you dodged bullets and dove under swords?

190. On a dare, you attempted to climb down into the deep pit behind the school. After you've climbed about 30 feet, your rope snaps and you tumble an additional 20 feet below to the ground. When you come to, you find yourself standing outside of a ghostly, underground amusement park. What happens next?

CHAPTER 2: PEOPLE AND CREATURES

Winners and Losers

191. What is your greatest triumph of all time? What circumstances led to your success and how did such a victory make you feel right after you achieved it?

192. What is your greatest defeat? What did you learn from such a landmark loss? How will those lessons help you going forward?

193. If you could choose to win a championship or other award in any sport or profession, which one would you choose and why?

194. When you play games or sports, are you more interested in having fun or winning and why? What do you think that says about you?

195. Discuss a time in which you encountered a sore loser. What was the activity you lost at and how did this sore loser make you feel bad for losing? How did you react to the teasing?

196. As the old saying goes, how you play the game is much more important than winning or losing. What do you think that means? How might you be able to "play the game" better going forward?

197. You are stepping up to the plate with two outs in the bottom of the ninth of an important baseball game. You will decide the winner and loser of this heated contest. What happens next?

198. What is an activity you participate in that you don't mind losing at? What keeps you from being more competitive at the activity? How does playing for fun make you feel?

199. What are some personality traits that can be found in a winner? What traits can be found in a loser? How do they differ and how do they overlap?

200. Following a major mix-up, you've been blamed by your entire city for the local sports team's playoff defeat. How do strangers treat you after blaming you for the loss? Would your family members treat you differently

too? Why or why not?

Brothers and Sisters

201. What qualities would make a perfect brother? If you have a brother, what keeps him from reaching this ideal? If you don't have a brother, write down a conversation between you and your imaginary brother.

202. Do you know anyone with an extremely good relationship with his or her sister? If so, how do you think they are able to get along so well? If not, what do you think it might take for a pair of siblings to enjoy each other's company?

203. What is the nicest thing your brother or sister has ever done for you? Why did he or she do it and how did it make you feel?

204. Brothers and sisters tend to be protective of one another. Describe a time when you've witnessed this overprotectiveness with your siblings or between siblings of another family. Do you think the protectiveness was appropriate? Why or why not?

205. What is the most annoying thing that your brother or sister has ever done to you? Why did it bother you so much? If you don't have a sibling, make up a situation with a really annoying squirt of a brother or sister.

206. How does the relationship between two siblings differ from the relationship between two good friends? How are the two sets of relationship similar?

207. Imagine you could trade your brother or sister for a cousin or a friend's sibling. Who would you trade your sibling for and why? Would you ever miss your actual brother or sister? Why or why not?

208. What do you think it's like to be a regular brother or sister of a celebrity or famous politician? How would you feel if you were in that situation?

209. Five years ago, you and your partner gave birth to a beautiful girl and boy, a set of fraternal twins. They have always hated each other and you have to deal with it every day. How do you get this brother and sister pair to get along?

210. How do you think your relationships with your siblings will change as you grow older? Why might the way you relate change over time?

Role Models

211. Who would your family members label as the worst role model in your life? Would you agree with them? Why or why not?

212. Who would you say has influenced you the most positively during your life? Do you think you influenced your role model back at all? Why or

why not?

213. Do you think a troubled person could improve their life completely with the use of a good role model? Why or why not?

214. What are some of the flaws your role model might have? Is this person still able to be your role model despite the flaws? Why or why not?

215. Who in your life could you be a role model toward? Do you think you'd have a positive influence? Why or why not?

216. People get role models from all sorts of places, even from the fictional world! What TV, movie or book character would you consider a role model? What are some lessons you might learn from this character?

217. For the low, low price of $1 million, you could make any celebrity into your role model. Do you think any celebrity would be worth that price? Why or why not?

218. Which of the following professions would make the best role models and why: professional basketball player, politician, CEO of a major corporation, or cardiac surgeon?

219. Create your role model dream team of authors, friends and famous people. How could you use their wisdom and words to live your ideal life?

220. Imagine that your biggest role model has gone to jail for a terrible crime. Would you still look up to this person? Why or why not?

Teachers

221. If you were a teacher, what subject would you teach and why? How long do you think it would take you to get the hang of it and why?

222. What do you think are three major challenges of teaching? How would you try to overcome such challenges as a teacher and would you be successful? Why or why not?

223. Did you ever have a teacher who had no idea what they were doing? What was it that made the teacher so clueless? How did having a teacher like that make you feel and why?

224. Who is your favorite teacher of all time and why? What are some lessons you've learned from this all-star teacher?

225. Imagine that your school acted as both a learning institution and as an apartment complex where all of your teachers lived and hung out. How would your teachers interact while cooking dinner, sharing a bathroom, and tidying up after themselves?

226. What is the toughest school subject you've ever had to learn? How did the teacher help or hinder your learning? Was the class a success? Why or why not?

227. Imagine that you had to teach something to a friend or a peer. How would you go about making sure this person learned everything possible about the subject? Would this experience make you empathize with your

school teachers? Why or why not?

228. What traits are most important for an effective teacher? How would cultivating those traits in yourself help you to learn or work?

229. If you could choose any person in the world to be your mentor, who would it be and why? What do you think you'd learn and how would you apply those skills?

230. If you could teach your teachers three key things, what would they be and why? Do you think they'd ever listen? Why or why not?

Insects

231. As part of a game show, you have been locked in a room filled with the insect that scares you the most. What insect is it and why? How do you survive one hour in the room so you can win fabulous prizes?

232. If you could have any insect as a pet, which one would it be and why? How would people react to you having an insect as a pet?

233. What would life be like if human society resembled an ant colony? What role would you serve in this new society and why?

234. After a science experiment gone wrong, insects have started to take over the world! How will you and your friends stop the insect takeover and save the world?

235. With your flyswatter poised and ready to attack, the fly on the wall begins pleading for his life! How do you react? Would you still kill the fly? Why or why not?

236. If you could be any insect for a few minutes, which insect would you choose and why? What would you do during your tiny, fast-moving time and why?

237. How would your life be different if people had to get into cocoons to grow to full size like a butterfly? What would you do while you were stuck in the cocoon?

238. There you were, a slow, crawling insect, just minding your own business. That's when the bird saw you and started to chase you! How will you escape from the bird's clutches?

239. Do you think all bugs are gross? Why or why not? What is it about insects that make people find them disgusting?

240. How do you think insects look at humans? Are we more scared of them or vice versa and why?

Birds

241. You are a bird flying high through the sky! What activities do you do that humans can't and why do you do them?

242. Many birds migrate south during the winter. If you had to leave

your home during the coldest part of the year, where would you go and why?

243. After a secret FBI experiment gone wrong, birds have become smarter than humans and have taken over the world! Which birds would be the most powerful and why?

244. Parrots have the ability to repeat certain phrases. If you owned a parrot, what would you be afraid for it to repeat to people that come to your home?

245. If you had to choose between being a human and a bird, which would you choose and why?

246. If you could fly with the greatest of ease, where would you go and what would you see? Who would you take with you on your flying journey and why?

247. What is your favorite type of bird and why? In what ways are you similar and different to your favorite feathered friend?

248. Birds never pack a change of clothes. If you had to wear the same clothes every day, what outfit would you choose and why?

249. Have you ever had a negative experience with a bird? If so, write down the details of that event. If not, make one up.

250. If you could make a movie about birds, what kinds of birds would be the characters and why? Is there one type of bird that makes a good villain? Why or why not?

Aliens

251. After seeing a strange light fly over your house on three consecutive nights, a loud noise and a ship landing have unwittingly made you the ambassador to a new race of alien life forms! What is your first encounter like? How do you ensure a peaceful existence between humans and aliens?

252. Bored with your current life, you stow away aboard a spaceship with a homemade space suit. When the ship docks at a space station, you come out of hiding to find a surprise. There aren't just humans, but dozens of alien races just walking or flying about normally. What happens next in your secret space station adventure?

253. Do you believe humanity will ever encounter an alien life form? If so, will it be more of a diplomatic encounter like Star Trek, violent like Independence Day, or something completely different? Why?

254. There you were, just minding your own business, and all of a sudden you were beamed up into a UFO. You prepare mentally for what you assume will be a probing situation. You're surprised to see a sort of alien psychologist walk in, wanting to ask a few questions in English. What does this well-educated alien want to know from you and why?

255. In the movie *Men in Black*, some people living on Earth were designated as aliens in disguise. Who that you know personally and who in the celebrity would do you think are most likely to be extraterrestrials? Write a story in which you find out some of their secret identities.

256. There was no invasion, just an immigration of thousands of aliens to our planet. All of a sudden, we were learning their language, playing their games and generally assimilating their culture into ours. What is it about their way of life we find so fascinating? Will they ever truly blend into our world?

257. You and the love of your life go running off into a field together, kissing and whispering sweet nothings into each other's ears. Your partner asks if you can keep a secret before revealing, under a human mask, that your love is actually an alien! Your partner asks you to run away from Earth to live a life of love. What do you decide? Will your love for your alien partner remain the same?

258. The invasion has begun and it seems that nobody is truly safe. The aliens have technology that is far superior to our own and it's only our resilience that's keeping us alive at this point. How will you survive the attack and what will our race do to keep alive?

259. An unmanned ship has landed in our nation's capital. In it, we find scientific knowhow that is over 1,000 years advanced beyond our own. It includes vaccines against many "incurable" diseases, food and housing shortage solutions and a host of other technological remedies. This alien craft asks for only one thing in return. What is the request, do we comply, and what happens next?

260. The world has fallen ill to what seems like an alien virus that hailed from a recent mission to Mars. Those who die seem to return possessed by an alien captor and those who are immune are quickly enslaved. What is the Martian objective and will humanity be able to fight back?

Zombies

261. A virus has been let loose upon the world, and it is turning people into zombies! How does the virus work? How is it transferred? How do you go about stopping it?

262. Are you really afraid of an actual zombie threat? Why or why not?

263. If a friend of yours turned into a zombie, would you be able to fight him or her? Why or why not?

264. In what ways are zombies and mummies alike? In what ways are they different? Which are you more afraid of and why?

265. How would the world's various governments and militaries stop a zombie apocalypse? What would be the safest place on the planet to avoid

getting infected and why?

266. A zombie has bitten you and you only have a few minutes left of humanity! How does it feel to be a zombie once the virus takes hold? Do you still remember being a human? In what ways are you still like your old self, and in what ways are you completely different?

267. You meet a zombie that can talk and have rational thoughts. Also, he doesn't want to eat your brains. Do you befriend him? Why or why not?

268. Zombies have become a fascination for people ever since the late 1960s. Why do you think people are so intrigued by zombies? What do zombies have over other horrific creatures that catch people's attention?

269. Of all of your friends, who loves zombies the most and why? Would this friend actually be excited if there were a zombie attack? Why or why not?

270. In a new Hollywood movie, the following creatures are locked into a room together: a vampire, a werewolf, a zombie, and a robotic tiger. Who would win and why? What might the movie be called?

CHAPTER 3: THE BODY AND THE BRAIN

Fitness

271. Would you consider yourself a physically active person? Why or why not? Do you want to become more active? Why or why not?

272. If there was a cheap and easy way to become extremely athletic and fit, do you think it would be worth it? Why or why not? What value might you lose in not having to put in the hard work?

273. What is your preferred type of exercise and why? Do you have more fun doing this exercise alone or with others and why?

274. Imagine you have to go on a special diet to either lose weight or avoid an allergic reaction. How would your view of food change? What foods would you miss the most and why?

275. How important is fitness to you on a scale of "the couch is my friend" to "I can't live without it?" Do you think you'll always have the same viewpoint? Why or why not?

276. In many ways, the key to fitness is motivation. What is your #1 motivation to stay or get in shape and why? How could you motivate yourself even more in the future?

277. You've been cast as a superhero in a major motion picture! Before you can celebrate, you need to work out four hours a day and eat a very specialized diet to get in superhero shape. How would you handle putting so much time into your fitness? Is it worth it? Why or why not?

278. You are running your first marathon! Describe how you feel during the grueling event. What might have motivated you to take up this challenge?

279. You are working out at the gym and you see someone in much better shape right next to you. Does seeing this person motivate you to work harder or does he or she intimidate you? Why?

280. Obesity is a major issue, especially for kids. What do you think is causing this epidemic? What does all this obesity say about our society and why does it say that?

Illness and Injury

281. A new plague has broken out through the U.S., infecting millions of people! How do you avoid getting sick? Will scientists find a cure before it's too late? What happens next?

282. In a dark forest, you've tripped and fallen down a deep well. You're alive but badly injured. How would you try to save yourself? Would help arrive in time? Why or why not?

283. Describe a time in which you were the sickest you've ever been. How did you feel and how did the people around you take care of you? What precautions have you taken since then to avoid becoming as sick?

284. Describe the most injured you've ever been. What happened to cause the injury? How did you recover?

285. What are some of the ways in which you're limited when you don't feel well? How do you handle things emotionally when you feel that way?

286. What's the most serious injury you've ever seen live or on TV? What was your reaction to the injury? How would you be able to cope if the same thing happened to you?

287. How do you deal with people who are ill? Would you be a good caretaker or would you rather stay as far away as you can? Why?

288. If you weren't feeling well, who would you most want taking care of you and why? Who would you least want to take care of you and why?

289. Some people believe in healing illness and injury using prayer or the power of the mind. Do you believe that some healing takes place without medicine? Why or why not?

290. You've been placed in the hospital with an undiagnosable illness. Would you be scared? Why or why not? How would the doctors figure out how to cure you?

Puberty

291. Middle and high school are so jam-packed with puberty-related hormones it seems like awkwardness is waiting around every corner. Describe one such hormone-related embarrassing situation you've faced. What were the consequences of this awkward event?

292. In the game of puberty it seems as though the most gifted and quickest developers are typically the winners. Do you believe there is a trade-off for being such an early bloomer and if so, why? How has your life been impacted by you being an early, late, or normal bloomer?

293. While they're already pretty comedic and outdated on their own, write the script for a puberty instruction video to be shown to a room full of fifth or sixth graders. Make sure to use as much retro language (and clothing) as you can. Would this video have prepared you more or less than your actual school system did as a kid?

294. When did you first realize that you were going through puberty and how did it change the way you lived your life? If you could go back and live those first few hormonal years over again, how would you lead them differently and why?

295. Kids can be especially mean when they see someone going through a particularly awkward stage of puberty. Describe a situation you saw or that you could have seen involving this kind of teasing when you were growing up. What would the older you have said to those kids?

296. Puberty has changed over the last century, with hormones in food and other factors causing it to begin earlier. How will this younger onset of puberty affect kids and parents alike? What would your life have been like if you started pubescent development three years earlier?

297. You have been transported to a world in which puberty doesn't begin until adulthood. Up through the age of 20 or so, most kids remain small, obedient, and focused on their studies. How does this delayed development world work differently from our own? What are the benefits and detriments of such a scenario?

298. In some past and current cultures, getting married at a young age, even before puberty, was and is an acceptable practice. Write about how your puberty experience would have been different if you were already married during it.

299. Many people think back to their school days with regret about what they could have done differently in their romantic choices. The problem is, during that time, they didn't have the hindsight and wisdom of today, meanwhile their puberty hormones were keeping logic at bay. Why do these people get so caught up in negativity about these past transgressions or scenarios?

300. As has been seen in multiple cases of teachers dating students, some adults get confused about physical development and its relation to maturity. Are these people just mentally ill or does society play a part? What can be done to stop this dangerous correlation and conduct?

The Senses

301. If you were forced to give up one of your five senses, losing it forever, which one would you choose and why? How would your life change from your unfortunate sensory deprivation?

302. Some people have extremely strong vision or excellent hearing.

Which would you say is the strongest of your five senses? How have you used this stronger sense to your advantage? Which, in contrast, is your weakest sense?

303. Do you have any friends who are blind or hearing impaired? How do you think a person with this sensory lack has been able to function successfully in society? What difficulties must he or she overcome in a modern world?

304. After a freak accident at the ophthalmologist's office, you have gained superior sight, allowing you to focus on objects that are extremely far away. How will you utilize this new ability? Will you keep it secret or make an effort to somehow exploit your heightened sense for financial gain? How does this change affect your life?

305. The olfactory glands, which are used for smell, are the most directly connected to the brain of all the five senses. Describe a few separate occasions in which a smell brought you back to the memory of a person or a place. What smell do you think has the most emotional resonance in your memory?

306. Would you describe yourself as touchy feely with people, as having a large personal space area, or as somewhere in between? How did you develop this sense with people and how has your upbringing affected it?

307. What is the most disgusting, revolting thing you've ever eaten? Where were you when it happened, what led up to it, and what was the aftermath? How did this incident shape your palette for meals to come?

308. Describe a time in which your five senses deceived you. For instance, your eyes or ears might have played tricks on you with shadows or a creaking pipe. What did you think was happening nearby and what actually happened?

309. You have advanced to the finals of a food tasting competition with the grand prize being a cool million. During the contest, you must determine the ingredients and country of origin of each food you taste. Detail the finals from beginning to end. Do you win or not, and why?

310. A major sinus infection has caused you to go temporarily deaf. How will you effectively communicate with your friends and loved ones? How has this experience made you better appreciate your sense of hearing?

Body Image

311. What parts of your body do you not like and why? How has this distaste for a part of yourself affected your life?

312. What about your body do you really like? In what ways does this part of your appearance make you feel good about yourself and why?

313. When you look in the mirror, how do you usually react and why? Are you happy with the way you are or do you think you need a change,

and why?

314. Think back to a time in which you felt insecure about your body in front of other people. What might have been a way to keep your self-esteem high in that situation and why?

315. While walking down the street, a complete stranger starts to make fun of you for looking a certain way. How would you react and why? How would your family and friends want you to react?

316. If you could look like somebody else, who would you choose to look like and why? How would your first day in this new body be different and why?

317. Some people go to a lot of trouble to change their bodies through extreme diets and plastic surgery. Would you ever resort to such a decision? Why or why not?

318. Have you ever judged another person to feel better about yourself? Did you share your opinions or keep them to yourself? Why?

319. The owner of a magical potion shop has given you the ability to improve one thing about the way you look. What do you choose to change and why? Is it worth it? Why or why not?

320. What would you have to do to be perfectly content with your body image? In what ways would your life improve with this new viewpoint and why?

Age

321. During what age have you felt the most comfortable in your own skin? Would you be willing to go back to that age, knowing you'd lose all of the skills, knowledge, and wisdom you've accumulated since that point? Why or why not?

322. Have you ever had a close relationship with someone that was a drastically different age than you? What clicked and what didn't click between the two of you? What did you learn during that relationship?

323. Society says that certain things like marriage and having kids are supposed to happen at specific ages, but throughout time those ages have changed. Do you feel a particular need to conform to today's standards? Why or why not?

324. You have suddenly been transported back in time and back into the body of your first grade self. Despite your best efforts, you appear stuck and you'll essentially need to re-live your life. How do you treat these younger ages differently the second time around?

325. In a rough economy and an aging population it seems like people are retiring later in life, if they retire at all. What is your opinion about retirement and an age you should stop working, if that age exists? How do you envision your twilight years with respect to working?

326. How did people live their lives differently at your age, 30 years ago? How will people at that age change in the next 30 years? Why has the way people live at your age changed like that over time?

327. There are many age-related milestones like getting a permit to drive at 16, voting at 18, drinking at 21, etc. What do you feel like that most important age-connected event was for you and why? How does that compare with the opinions of your friends and loved ones?

328. Many people label high school and college dating relationships as immature and say that you won't find deep, lasting love until you reach the adult world. Do you think that opinion holds water and why or why not? At what age do you think that a person could viably find true love and why?

329. You've found a strange device at a garage sale that allows you to change any person into any age you choose for an entire day! How would you use this device in your life? What ages would you change your friends and family to? What age would you change yourself to and why?

330. Some people refer to themselves as a fine wine, getting better with age. Do you feel as though you're getting better with age? How could you increase how much "better" you with the passing years?

Anger

331. What are some things that make you angry? Which makes you the most angry and why? Would you describe your anger as rational or irrational, and why?

332. Describe a time when a friend or family member made you really angry. What made you so incensed and how were you able to resolve the situation?

333. While you may think you're perfect, some things you do may anger other people. What are a few examples of your more irritating traits? If those traits make other people angry, why do you still do them?

334. Do you think anger is ever a positive response to something? Why or why not? Describe a time when your anger may have helped you.

335. What typically happens when you make a decision based on anger? How can you ensure that you make fewer angry emotional decisions in the future?

336. What are some things you might do or say to calm down an angry friend? Do those things work in practice? Why or why not?

337. You've made a teacher or a boss very angry, but you aren't sure what you did. What happens next?

338. What do you think the world would be like if there was no anger? Would you rather life in a world like that? Why or why not?

339. The comic book character the Incredible Hulk turns into a giant, green rage monster when he gets angry. In what ways are you similar to the

Hulk when you get mad? In what ways are you different?

340. Think about someone you know who always makes you angry. Do you think this person deserves your anger? Why or why not? What if the tables were turned and this person was always angry at you? Would you deserve it? Why or why not?

Jealousy

341. Why do you think people become jealous? Do you think jealousy is common across different cultures? Why or why not?

342. What was the last time you became jealous? Who were you jealous of and why? How would you feel if you found out that person was jealous of you?

343. How might you act differently toward a person if you were jealous of them? How would this person act differently toward you if they found out you were jealous?

344. You've achieved your wildest dreams of fame and fortune! Now, many of your friends are jealous of your success. How will this change your relationships with them and why?

345. Do you ever envy celebrities? If so, who in particular are you jealous of and why? If not, why do you think some people are so obsessed with the lives of famous folks?

346. One of your best friends in the world is dating your biggest crush and you are jealous beyond belief. How do you handle the situation without harming your friendship? Would the situation change your relationship? Why or why not?

347. What might be some good life advice to give to someone who wanted to stop being so jealous of people? Would you be able to apply some of that advice to yourself? Why or why not?

348. Which of the following people would you be most jealous of and why: a lottery winner, People's sexiest man or woman, the smartest person alive, or a professional athlete?

349. What is the first time you can remember ever being jealous of someone else? How do you think this new feeling changed you? Did your envy have any negative consequences? Why or why not?

350. Which of your family members are you the most jealous of and why? Have you always been jealous of him or her? How might this feeling change over time?

Kindness

351. What is it that makes people want to be kind? Would you consider yourself a person who wants to be kind to others? Why or why not?

352. Who would you say is the kindest person you know? How do you think he or she is able to be kind in a world that can be very unkind?

353. Imagine a world where kindness has been outlawed. How would people act differently? Would your day-to-day life change significantly? Why or why not?

354. How does it make you feel when you're kind to others? What are some opportunities in your life to be more kind to your friends and loved ones?

355. Do you think that most people are kind for the sake of being kind, or for selfish reasons? Why do you feel that way? When you're kind to others, is it selfless or selfish and why?

356. After finding a highlighted passage in a magical spell book, you can now turn one person of your choosing into the kindest human being on earth. Who would you choose to use this spell on and why? How would this person's life change?

357. What is the kindest thing someone else has ever done for you? Describe the experience and how it made you feel. Did you ever tell this person how much the act meant to you? Why or why not?

358. What is the kindest thing you've ever done for someone else? How did it make you feel and why? How did the other person react to your kindness?

359. Do you think it means more to do something kind for a friend or a complete stranger? Why do you feel this way?

360. In what ways are you kind or unkind to yourself? Why do you think having a positive attitude toward yourself might be important?

Belief

361. Do you usually believe in yourself? Why or why not? Why might it be important to have faith in yourself and what you can accomplish?

362. Imagine that you've come across the most gullible person alive who will believe anything you say. What might you try to tell him or her? Would you feel bad if you made them believe something extremely crazy? Why or why not?

363. What do you think is the most important aspect of having something to believe in? What might a person miss out on by not believing in something greater than him- or herself and why?

364. You've gained the ability to make anything happen just by believing in it! How would you use this power? How might your friends and family treat you differently after they see you use your power?

365. What would you consider to be your greatest belief? Why do you believe it? How do your loved ones feel about that belief?

366. What helps you believe that you can achieve your dreams? How

will you maintain that belief going forward?

367. What is something that you have trouble believing in? Why do you find it unbelievable? How do people usually try to convince you to believe?

368. You've just seen an alien spaceship land in your backyard. How do you convince your friends to believe the incredible sight? Do they continue to doubt your claims? Why or why not?

369. Have you ever had to convince someone to believe in you? If so, what did you have to do to make people believe in your trustworthiness? If not, make up a story in which you have to convince multiple people to follow your point of view.

370. How would your life be different if you were a very believable liar? How would you feel about yourself after applying this ability to your everyday life?

Dreams

371. You've just witnessed it: the end of the world. These kind of dreams are the ones you like to push out of your mind, but there's only one problem. Everything that happened in the beginning of your dream, from your trip to work to your conversations with co-workers, are word-for-word in line with the apocalyptic dream you just had. What happens next and what do you do about it?

372. Imagine that you had the chance to get your "dream" everything. Your dream job. Your dream partner. Your dream house. What would it be like if everything and person in your life was dreamily ideal? How would your typical day change?

373. Think back to all of your most memorable dreams and single out the scariest recurring dream you ever had. What do you think it symbolized? If you had complete control over the dream, how do you think you would have conquered such a fearful night of slumber?

374. Martin Luther King, Jr. had a dream that all people, regardless of race and creed, could come together as one. If you were placed behind a podium in front of thousands of people with the entire world watching, what do you think your dream would be for a better tomorrow and why?

375. Upon working for a mad scientist, you realize that you've been helping him to create a device that lets you go into other people's dreams! You take the technology out for a test drive one night. Whose dreams do you go into and what do you do while you're in there?

376. We've all had them and whether or not we talk about them, we probably enjoy our naughty dreams thoroughly. Describe your first risqué dream, why you think you had it, and what your reaction was afterward. Did it cause you to feel happy, ashamed or a completely different emotion?

377. The world has been plunged into one large collective dream, with

every person having the ability to control everything that affects his own skills, appearance, and persona, but with no control over other people. How would this new order of things change your life in particular?

378. Have you ever had a dream that felt so completely real, you even convinced yourself that it was reality? What felt so genuine about the dream and what do you remember the most about it? What would it take for such an event to happen in real life?

379. Joseph, famous for his Technicolor dream coat, was also a killer dream interpreter. List five of your most confusing dreams and do your best to write an explanation of what they might mean. Which of these dream interpretations is the most important to your life and why?

380. Imagine that in your dream you could have a one-on-one meeting with the true inner-you: your subconscious. You can ask this inner-you any questions you want to find out about your identity, your desires, and your destiny. What questions do you ask and how does your subconscious respond?

Fears

381. Name five things that you are personally afraid of in order of most fearful to least. Why are you afraid of those things in particular? What would change about your life if you conquered those fears? How do you think you'd be able to do it?

382. Think back to a time when your fears prevented you from doing something you wanted to do. For example, after all of your friends jumped off the high rock platform, you wanted to prove yourself but couldn't because of fear. Do you think that your fear helped or hurt you in that instance and why?

383. Imagine that you were alive in ancient times with your same fight or flight response having to battle the perilous dangers of the uncivilized world. Do you think that you would be successful facing such scary challenges or that you would be too modernized to stand much of a chance?

384. List five different phobias that you've heard of or try to make a few up. Write a little story for each about how your life would be different if you had that particular phobia. What normal activities might you not be able to participate in due to your clinical fears?

385. As you're walking down the street you come upon a mirror that makes you look about 20 years older. Suddenly, you realize it's not a mirror, but it's actually you from the future, coming to help you face your greatest fears to avoid a later-in-life calamity! What does this future self help you with and are the two of you successful?

386. Was there ever someone during elementary, middle, or high school

whom you were genuinely afraid of? Imagine that you have come face to face with this person during a situation in which you couldn't leave the room and had to talk to him or her for an extended period of time. What would happen and would you continue to remain afraid after the encounter?

387. A lot of people are more afraid of death than they are anything else. Why do you think so many people list death as their number-one fear? Where do you rank it in the fears of your life and how do you think the fear of death has shaped who you are today?

388. For those who are afraid of public speaking, the time-honored suggestion of picturing the audience in their underwear has been made over and over again. If you had to add any other tips to someone who was afraid of speaking to a room, what would they be and how have you used them to your own benefit?

389. In the *Nightmare on Elm Street* movie series, an evil and scorned former school employee attacks students in their sleep by bringing their worst fears to life. What would your encounter with such a freaky individual be like and which of your fears would spring at you in a deadly fashion?

390. How would the world be different if humans had a constant fight or flight response to any stimulus, much like birds or insects? How would your day be different if you were scared of anything and everything around you all the time?

Goals

391. Imagine that you could go back five years, insert a series of amazing and difficult long-term goals and achieve them by the present day. What about your life would be different with those goals having been achieved? Now, what are some goals you have for five years down the line and how will your life change after having made them a reality?

392. Think about the most goal-oriented person you know. List some of the accomplishments this person has been able to make a reality for him- or herself. How do you think this person was able to focus so successful on these goals and what would you have to do to have the same level of success for yourself?

393. It's been said that if you don't create your own goals, someone else will create them for you. For example, if you don't create a weight or body image goal for yourself, your goal might be taken over by the Photoshop-heavy media. What are some goals in your life that you didn't put there yourself and with what other goals would you like to replace them?

394. Goals don't always have to be something as big as an Olympic Gold Medal or a novel. They might simply represent a tiny step you take each day for your health, your home, or your relationships. What are five

tiny, little goals that you could add to your life and how would you achieve them step-by-step?

395. Motivational speaker Brian Tracy has said that one of the most effective ways to improve goal setting is to write them down each day to engrave them into your subconscious. Do you think this idea holds water? Imagine if you tried such a practice for 30 days and write a story about your goal-setting success or failure.

396. After an odd encounter with a fallen spaceship, you have been granted the ability to make all of your goals come true as soon as you think of them. They don't magically appear, but you can pretty much put yourself on autopilot as your seemingly possessed body takes care of all the hard work involved. How much more successful would you be if you could so easily get the tough stuff out of the way and simply reap the rewards?

397. Have you ever had a time in your life when someone told you something was impossible...and then you proved them wrong? Describe such an event or make one up in which you worked so hard for a seemingly unattainable goal that you practically willed it into being.

398. What is the hardest goal you can think of that you just might be able to achieve if you had unlimited resources and time? What kind of things would you have to do on a daily basis and what aspects of it would you need an extreme amount of help with? How would you feel after achieving it?

399. Think of four or five friends you've had over the years who have had or currently have goals that line up quite well with yours. Who of those friends, including yourself, has been the most successful at achieving those goals. What would you have to do to be the most successful out of the lot of them?

400. In an amazing technological breakthrough, a scientist has created a goal computer that allows you to type in any goal and it will tell you without guess work exactly what you need to do to achieve it. The computer calculates every single step of the process from beginning to end. How would such a device help you to progress with your own goals?

Guts

401. Think of a time when you were brave when it would have been easy to walk away from a challenge. How did your courage make you feel and why? How would you have felt differently if you'd been more cowardly?

402. Who is someone you know who shows a lot of guts in his or her everyday life? What about them makes them brave and how do they show this bravery?

403. Who is a TV, movie, or book character that you would describe as

a total coward? What would this character have to do to show more guts and why?

404. There are times to be brave and there are times to be careful. What is a situation in which the best thing that a person could do is run away? Would you run away in that situation? Why or why not?

405. When in your life have you worked up the nerve to take a risk? What was the risk and how did things turn out for you?

406. Who in your family would you describe as brave? How would this family member's life be different if he or she were a coward and why?

407. What are some fears in your life that you have overcome? What are the three best ways for people to get over their fears and why do they work?

408. Your best friend has been kidnapped by mole people! How do you muster up the courage to help your friend? What happens when you try to save your friend?

409. Think back to a time when you could have been brave but you allowed your fear to control you. Do you regret your actions? Why or why not? Would you make the same choice again?

410. Sometimes admitting our mistakes takes guts. What is a mistake that you have openly admitted to? How did you feel once you admitted this error and why?

Confidence

411. Would you consider yourself a confident person? If so, what are the situations in which you feel super-confident and why are they no sweat for you? If not, how would you go about getting a confidence makeover?

412. What are some good things to do when you need a confidence boost? Why might those actions help you?

413. What activity in your life requires the most confidence? How does it suffer when you aren't feeling very sure of yourself?

414. You've won an online auction for a super confidence-boosting serum that lasts for 24 hours. When would you take this concoction and what would you do to take advantage of your supercharged self-esteem?

415. Who would you consider to be the most confident person you know? How does he or she compare to the least confident person you know? What could they learn from one another?

416. Do you think confidence is an important part of leading a successful life? Why or why not?

417. What kinds of things bring your confidence level down? How might you be able to avoid such occurrences, going forward?

418. Of all the things you do in your life, what would you say you're the most confident at and why? How would you feel if you could do that activity for a living and why?

419. What do you think is the difference between being confident and being cocky? Do you think it's okay to be cocky every so often? Why or why not?

420. What is an activity you'd like to become more confident at? Detail a plan of action to become extremely confident at this activity. How long would it take and how would you feel after accomplishing it?

Stress

421. When you're at your most stressed, where is a place you can go to calm down? What is it about this location that makes you feel better? Would you recommend it to others? Why or why not?

422. What do you think are the most stressful events you'll endure in your entire life? How will these events compare with the stressors you've already dealt with?

423. During a massive earthquake, you've been locked in a room with the three people you know who handle stress the worst. How will you deal with these extremely stressed individuals? Will you be able to calm them down? Why or why not?

424. What is an example of an activity in your life that causes you stress that you continue to do anyway? Why do you enjoy the activity despite the stress?

425. Of all the people in the world, who would you say stresses you out the most? If you had to work closely with this person, how would you try to keep your stress in check? Would you be successful? Why or why not?

426. What are some ways that people might be able to tell that you're stressed out? What do people typically tell you when they figure out that you're stressed? Do their suggestions help? Why or why not?

427. While distress is thought of as a negative type of stress, eustress is a positive form of stress. What do you think the difference is between the two? When is a time that you've experienced eustress in your life?

428. How would your life change if you never felt stress? Would this be a positive or a negative change and why?

429. What is something you have to do every day that causes you stress? How might you go about making this task less stressful? How would you feel if you were successful?

430. Think back to the most stressful time in your life. How does thinking about this event make you feel? What would you do differently if you had to go through this all over again?

CHAPTER 4: CONCEPTS

Teamwork

431. Are you an effective team leader? Why or why not? How could you get better?

432. Would you consider yourself a better leader or a better follower and why? Does a strong team need both? Why or why not?

433. Write about a situation in your life you had to face alone. How do you think having a team behind you would have helped?

434. What are some of the toughest parts of working on a team and why? Describe how you've faced these issues when you've been on a team.

435. When a sports team wins a championship, it's usually a team effort. What are some important aspects of a championship team that might be ignored in favor of the best players? Do you think the lesser-recognized players would ever get jealous? Why or why not?

436. If you were working on an important project, who would be on your dream team and why? Who would be on that team if you could pick from famous people you don't know?

437. It's been said that one of the secrets to a good relationship is being "on the same team." What do you think that means? Have you seen that concept in action? Why or why not?

438. Think of a time when you had difficulty working on a group. Why didn't the group work? Were you at all to blame? Why or why not?

439. You have been appointed as the manager of a team of superheroes like the Avengers! How do you keep these egotistical and mighty people in the team mindset? Are you able to conquer a well-oiled team of supervillains? Why or why not?

440. What do you think you'd be able to accomplish if you had a whole team behind you at all times and why?

Being Alone

441. Which person in your group of friends has the hardest time being alone? Why do you think this person always needs other people around?

442. Would you prefer being alone or in a large group of people and why? What is your ideal number of people to be around and why?

443. What is your favorite thing to do alone? Why would you rather do this activity alone than with other people?

444. The phrase "I need to be alone" is practically a cliché. Describe a time when it would be appropriate for a person to be alone. Have you ever been in that kind of situation? How did it feel and why?

445. After locking yourself in a safe during the apocalypse, you are the last person on planet Earth! How do you survive? How do you cope with being completely alone for the rest of your days?

446. If you had a choice between never finding love or settling for someone to avoid being alone, which would you choose and why? Do you think a lot of people make this choice? Why or why not?

447. Are you afraid of being alone? Why or why not?

448. A person has been discovered living in the wilderness for their entire life! You are in charge of teaching them how to exist in society. What troubles would this person have in adapting to being around other people? How will you help them to adjust?

449. Some people talk about needing "alone time." How much alone time do you need every day or week? Why is this amount of time right for you?

450. Describe a time when you felt lonelier than you'd ever felt before. What happened that made you feel so lonely? How did you snap out of it?

Loss

451. When in your life have you experienced great loss? What was this time like for you and why?

452. How do you think people will experience loss when you pass away? How might they act during your funeral? Who would deliver your eulogy and why?

453. Imagine that a person who was very close to you passed away. How might this person's death make you feel? Would you make any changes in your life as a result of the death? Why or why not?

454. If you had to console someone experiencing great loss, how would you do so and why? Do you think you helped this person? Why or why not?

455. Do you feel like there are any parts of yourself you've lost over the years? If so, how did you lose this part of yourself? Was it for the best?

Why or why not?

456. Sometimes, we don't learn to appreciate something until it is gone. Have you ever experienced this? Why do you think you took this thing for granted?

457. What do you think would help you the most if you were experiencing grief and why? What would help you the least and why?

458. After casting a magical spell, you have the ability to reconnect with any friend or loved one, living or deceased, for as long as you want. Who would you choose and why? How would this reconnection make you feel and why?

459. Which person in your life are you the most afraid to lose and why? How would this loss affect you and why?

460. If you had to give advice to someone experiencing loss, what would it be and why? Would you be able to take your own advice? Why or why not?

Secrets

461. We all keep secrets. What is a secret that you have kept? How has this secret affected you and those around you?

462. Your country needs the greatest secret agent in the world – in other words, you. The CIA has sent you on a vital mission to another country. What is your mission and why are you the right person for the job?

463. You have been captured by aliens! They are probing your brain for secrets. What secrets are you afraid of them finding out and why?

464. Superheroes often have secret identities. What would it be like to keep your true identity a secret? Why might you have to hide who you really are?

465. Your best friend reveals an intense secret to you. What is the secret and what is your response?

466. Everywhere you go, people are whispering behind your back about you. What do you do to find out what they're saying? What are they saying and how does it affect you?

467. You just found out that your boss is secretly working for the mafia! Will you turn him or her in or keep your mouth shut and reap the rewards? Why?

468. You've just tattled on someone at school or work and you got this person in major trouble. Do you feel bad? Why or why not?

469. A major secret has been gnawing at you and you finally unburden it on someone else. Who would you share a deep, dark secret with? How does telling it make you feel?

470. Not all secrets are bad. What is a secret that you keep hidden that makes you happy? Why does keeping this a secret bring you joy?

Success and Failure

471. What is the greatest success that you have achieved in your life? What good came out of it and why?

472. What is your greatest failure? How has it affected you personally? What would you have to do to let it go?

473. What are some of the key differences between the most successful person you know and the biggest failure? What would happen if they switched places and why?

474. If you could achieve any success that you wanted, what would it be and why? Why is this goal so important to you? How would you go about achieving this objective?

475. Failure is a big fear for most people. What is something that you are terrified of failing at? Why do you think that you might not succeed?

476. Small victories that occur every day can increase a person's self-esteem. What is a minor thing that you succeed at that makes you feel good about yourself? Why does it make you feel accomplished?

477. Sometimes failure can be a lesson in how to succeed in the future. What is something that you once failed at that you learned to do better? What are some current issues for you that you might be able to tackle in the future?

478. Think of a major goal that you achieved. How would your life be different if you had failed to achieve it? Why was this success so important to shaping your future?

479. Imagine an upcoming challenge. What is the challenge and how difficult will it be to succeed at the challenge? Will your success or failure make an impact on your life? Why or why not?

480. Stress can be a strong motivator or a crippling handicap. Which one is it for you and why? Is it better to have a completely stress-free environment, a stressful environment or one with a mix and why?

Habits

481. What is one of your daily habits? Would you consider this habit good or bad? How would your life change if you stopped doing it and why?

482. If you were forced to give up a habit, which one would be the hardest to do without and why?

483. Imagine your perfect daily routine in which you get to do everything you want. Describe the routine. Would this new routine lead to a happier and healthier you? Why or why not?

484. If you could pick up a habit from one family member, what would it be and why? In what ways would it improve your life? Would that family member mind your mimicry?

485. You wake up one day to find yourself in another person's body. How is this person's daily routine different from your own? Would you be able to adjust to this new life? Why or why not?

486. What is your worst habit? Why do you continue to do it? How does the habit make your loved ones feel and why?

487. What is your healthiest habit? How did you start doing it? How will this habit improve your life going forward?

488. Think of an annoying habit that one of your friends has. What is the habit and why is it so annoying? How could you get this person to stop the irritating habit?

489. Imagine that you lived 100 years in the past. In what ways would your habits have to change for you to live at that time? How difficult would it be to change your ways to fit into this culture?

490. What is an old habit that you once did that you no longer do? Why did you stop doing it? How would you instruct someone else on getting rid of that habit?

Good and Evil

491. What separates a good person from a bad person? What are some elements both good and bad people have in common?

492. You find yourself in a compromising position. There is something that you really want to do, but there is something else that you *should* do. Describe the situation. What do you decide to do and why?

493. Imagine a person who is completely evil. What would happen if this person became the supreme ruler of the whole planet? What would this evil person do? How would you help to stop him or her?

494. How do you think the world would be if we were all completely good people? How would people act differently? Is this a kind of world you'd want to live in? Why or why not?

495. Good usually triumphs over evil, but not always. When has evil triumphed over good in your life? What might you do next time to make sure good wins out and why?

496. You meet two wizards. One of them is incredibly evil, and the other is extremely noble and good. They each ask to take you on as an apprentice. How do they try to woo you? Which one is more convincing and why?

497. You are the leader of a very important cause that could help countless people to lead better lives. But you have to cheat to succeed. What do you decide to do? Do the ends justify the means?

498. How should people decide on the concepts of good and evil: what society says to do, using your own instincts, following religious teachings or something else? Which methods do you use the most and the least? Why?

499. Think of a group of people you perceive as evil or corrupt. Now imagine that you're one of them. Can you find the good in these people? If so, does it change your opinion about them?

500. Would your morals change if you were in a life or death situation? What would be different if you or your loved ones were at risk and why?

Wants and Needs

501. What are the main differences between wants and needs? Have you ever had trouble telling the difference?

502. What do you need the most in this world and why? Do you think there are a lot of people with similar needs? Why or why not?

503. Genie in a bottle! This genie is willing to give you three wishes. Would you wish for things that you needed or would they be things that you merely want and why?

504. If money, time and logistics weren't an issue, what would you want more than anything else and why?

505. Think of a time when you were forced to give up something that you wanted in order to have something that you needed. Why did you have to make this sacrifice? How did this situation make you feel?

506. Is it more satisfying to save up your money to get something you want or to get it immediately bought for you by your friends or parents? Why?

507. You meet a person from another planet. What kind of wants and needs does this alien creature compared to human beings? How will you help this alien to get what it needs?

508. Do we need different things than we did 100 years ago? Why or why not? How have these changing needs affected society?

509. You are stuck babysitting a kid who wants everything and he wants it now! How do you appease this child during your four-hour babysitting session? Are the child's parents happy with your solution? Why or why not?

510. What is something that you wanted badly but were unable to get? How would your life have changed if you received it? Would you have been satisfied or wanted something else right away and why?

Luxury

511. Would you say that you own more luxury items or necessities? Do you think it's important to own some items you don't really need? Why or why not?

512. If you had a choice between living a life of luxury and a life wherein you only had a few possessions to speak of, which would you choose and why? Would anybody you know make the opposite choice? Why would he

or she decide differently?

513. You've won the lottery and you can buy as many expensive items you want! What do you decide to buy with your winnings? Do you think these items will bring you happiness? Why or why not?

514. Do you envy people with a more luxurious lifestyle than you? Why or why not? What might you have that they're missing?

515. What do you think is more important and why: love or luxury? Do you think it's possible to have both? Why or why not?

516. You've been stranded on a deserted island with a plane's worth of items from a luxury Sky Mall catalogue. What items might help you to survive and why? How will you use these items to make sure you can be found?

517. People who live a luxurious lifestyle either have a lot of money or a lot of secret debt. If you wanted a life of luxury, what do you think you'd have to do as a career choice and why?

518. What are some reasons to avoid a luxurious life? Do you think a person working 80 hours a week in a high-paying job would be willing to listen to your advice? Why or why not?

519. If you had to go with only the bare necessities of food, clothing and shelter for an entire month, would you be able to handle it? Why or why not? Who in your family would have the hardest time surviving such a challenge and why?

520. Many people who acquire a lot of objects of luxury are surprised to find out that the items don't give them much joy. Why do you think that is? Do you think the best things in life are free? Why or why not?

Safety

521. We are taught at a very young age that safety is important. What safety tips have your family members given you? What was the best advice and why?

522. When you're scared, where do you to feel safe? Describe this place from top to bottom. Why does this place make you feel protected from the outside world?

523. Some people like to think certain reassuring thoughts when they're nervous. What is your mental safe place? Why might certain thoughts make people feel safer?

524. What activity do you do that requires the most safety equipment or training? What is so dangerous about this activity? Do you think all the safety stuff is necessary? Why or why not?

525. What's the most dangerous thing you've ever done? What about this activity made it unsafe? Would you do it again? Why or why not?

526. Imagine that your family was so scared for your safety that they put

you in a giant plastic bubble. What would your life be like as a guy or girl in a bubble? Would you actually be safer? Why or why not?

527. If you were into extreme sports, which one would you most like to try and why? What would your friends think about your wild and dangerous new ways?

528. There can be safety in numbers. What is a place that you would only go to in a group? Why would you never go alone?

529. If you were to travel to a foreign country, which country would you feel safest visiting? Which would be the least safe and why?

530. Your best friend has started to take major safety risks every single day. What are some of the risks and how do you help him or her to stay safe?

Humanity

531. What do you believe separates humans from other animals and why? What are some ways in which humans and other animals are similar?

532. What do you believe drive humans the most: our instincts or our rational thoughts and why do you believe that? What is the point of having rational thoughts?

533. The course of history has been changed and a different species evolved to be dominant on the planet. Which species is now the ruler of the planet? How would your day-to-day life be different in this new world?

534. What do you think it means to be human and why? What might an animal think it means to be human?

535. Do you believe that a person can perform an act so terrible that he or she ceases to be human? If so, what kind of act would this be and how would you personally look on this person?

536. What do you believe will be humanity's next great triumph? Why do you believe that this will be of great significance for the whole of humanity?

537. For all the good parts of humanity, we have done our share of evil as well. War and tragedy have both centered around human existence for ages. What drives humanity to war with itself?

538. Imagine that you were born thousands of years ago in a war between two tribes. How might your concept of humanity differ from the one you have today and why?

539. Humanity is not one big happy family. We are sectioned off into various nations. Why do you believe that we could not form one united nation under the same flag? Why must we exist apart?

540. You are the leader of one united human nation. What are some of your commands to ensure we live happily and healthily far into the future? How would you keep yourself from getting too greedy on the throne?

Gender

541. Historically, men were the rulers of most societies. What would a female-led society look like? Is this a civilization in which you'd want to live?

542. What are some non-obvious differences between men and women? How are men and women similar? Do you think the differences between men and women matter? Why or why not?

543. What would life be like if you had been born the opposite gender? What would be some of the differences in your activities, friendships and family relationships?

544. Women have fought for equal rights for a very long time. How would it feel to be part of a society in which you were a second-class citizen based on your gender?

545. What are your opinions on the issue of gender equality and why? Are your opinions the same or different than those of your family and friends?

546. What are some struggles that women face in contemporary society that men do not face? Do you think those struggles will change in the future? Why or why not?

547. Have you ever met a person who was transgender? If so, what was that encounter like and why? If not, describe a made-up story in which you meet a person whose body is one gender and whose mind and identity are the other.

548. How do you feel that men and women approach romance differently? Is one way better than the other? Why or why not?

549. Imagine that someone confused you for the opposite gender. How would it make you feel? Why?

550. You've decided to dress up as the opposite gender for one entire school year and you actually pull it off without getting discovered. What could you learn from such an experiment and why?

Popularity

551. Think back to a time when you felt like an outsider. How did it make you feel and why? What did you do to make your situation better?

552. You wake up one morning to find that overnight you have become the most popular kid in school! Everybody, from your close friends to the people that you once envied, treat you differently. How does it feel to be at the top of the school food chain? How does your new status make you behave differently?

553. No matter how hard you practice, your friends always pick you last in your favorite team sport. What would you do to stop being the last pick?

Could you still enjoy playing the game as the last pick? Why or why not?

554. You find a lamp in your backyard that has a genie inside of it! You desperately want to use the genie to make you more popular. What are three wishes you ask for to help you to achieve your goal? Do the wishes work? Why or why not?

555. Imagine that you are the ruler of an old and powerful nation. As the most important and popular person in your country, you have a lot of responsibilities and very little time for yourself. Describe your day-to-day life of royal popularity. Is all the popularity worth it, given how much work you have to do? Why or why not?

556. Is popularity important to you? Why or why not? Why do you think popularity is important to so many people?

557. You are a photographer of famous celebrities! Which celebrities do you normally photograph and what is it like following them around? Do you think they enjoy the attention? Why or why not?

558. Why is it that outward appearance seems to have a lot to do with popularity? Which is more important: what's on the inside or what's on the outside? Why?

559. You see someone being bullied, either verbally or physically, by the popular kids at school. What do you do? What are the consequences of your choice?

560. One day you run into an old classmate or former coworker. This person was once extremely popular and you envied this person. How has this person changed over the years? Do you still have reason to be envious? Why or why not?

Humor

561. How does your sense of humor relate to the sense of humor with the rest of your family? Which family member does your humor jibe with the most? Write a humorous sample dialogue between the two of you.

562. You have just won an award for being the funniest person in your school, workplace, or neighborhood. What aspects of your humor were so appealing to the judges? How will you be able to best defend your title from year to year?

563. Whether it be due to aging, maturity or the exposure to new comedic voices, our senses of humor tend to change over the years. How has your sense of humor changed over time and what caused it to morph? Has the change been for the better, why or why not?

564. You have found the partner of your dreams who is kind, loving, empathetic, and loyal. The only issue is that this person doesn't get your jokes at all, to the point that it sometimes feels like you're speaking different languages. Describe a typical comedic miscommunication between the two

of you. How will you overcome this silly issue?

565. Describe a time that your attempts at humor got you in trouble. Who did you rub the wrong way and how did you remedy the situation? What is another humor-related situation that could have offended someone even more gravely?

566. In a bit of poor scheduling, the two class clowns of the school have been parked right next to each other in English class. Describe their battle for comedic supremacy. Which clown's style will win out and why?

567. He's mean. He's sarcastic. And for some reason, all of your friends can't stop laughing at every word he says, even though he's often belittling and offending you in the process. During a long car ride with just the two of you, you finally confront him. What do you say to him and what is his response? Does the confrontation help in the long run?

568. You don't know when or how it happened, but somewhere along the way, your kids stopped thinking you were funny. What caused them to stop laughing at your jokes? Will you ever be able to get back into their comedic good graces?

569. Even though we attend events like comedic plays or raunchy rom-coms in hopes of laughing, it usually ends up being an unexpected scenario that causes you to laugh the most. Describe one of those unplanned comedic experiences that you can still chuckle about today. Why was it so amusing?

570. You have stumbled upon a secret warehouse of comedy. This is where all the comedic greats purchased their senses of humor, including Steve Martin, Woody Allen, and Louis C.K. You steal the comedic ability of one star in particular and use it as your own. Who do you choose, how do you utilize it, and why?

Politics

571. How would you describe yourself politically if you had to get extremely specific, beyond just simply party lines? How has your background and how have your circumstances shaped that set of beliefs? Do you think that you'd believe something different if you led a different life? Why or why not?

572. Do you have any friends who have a drastically different set of political beliefs than you do? Create a dialogue between you and one of those friends in which you come to the core of those political differences. Would having such a discussion affect your friendship negatively? Why or why not?

573. How does the subject of politics make an impact in your family? What would happen if your family had a heated political discussion at the Thanksgiving dinner table? Do you think you'll ever experience the same

situation 20, 40, or more years down the line with your progeny? Why or why not?

574. An advance by your time travel scientific research team has given you the ability to change the results of any presidential election in the past 100 years, but you can only do it once. Which election do you change and how does it effect the world?

575. How do you think the political landscape of the country will change in the next five years? What about the next 50? Why will it change in this way and will this change affect how you vote in future elections? What about the way your kids vote?

576. Imagine a world in which you had your own cable news channel stocked with shows hosted by your friends, family, and the people you respect. What would the focus of your network be, what would the shows be called and be about, and how successful do you think your station would be?

577. If you could work in politics, either for a candidate or as a candidate, with no limits of time or space, what time period would you pick to do it and why? Do you think you would be successful in the political biz or would you have certain shortcomings that slowed you down?

578. Have you ever personally met a politician? Relate or create a story in which you chatted with this political figure and what the two of you talked about. How did this conversation affect you and did it change or affirm your beliefs about typical politicians?

579. What is your opinion of political comedy, such as "The Daily Show" and "The Colbert Report?" Do you find it to be spot on or a blatant and inappropriate mockery of the system? What would you say to these well-studied comedians if you were interviewed on their programs?

580. There seems to be a lot of conspiracy theory on the outskirts of extremist politics. Much time is spent on birth certificates and far-out scandals while less time is spent on highlighting the day-to-day work of a political office. Are the media to thank for this or is it more the responsibility of the people? Will this trend grow or fade in the future?

The Environment

581. Imagine that you had the opportunity to walk through the United States over one thousand years ago before it had become industrialized in the slightest. What would it be like to breathe that air and how would the sky look at night? Was it worth all of the progress that civilization has made since that time? Why or why not?

582. There are so many issues of environmental problems in the world, it seems as though most people encounter them every single day. What are some issues you've witnessed first hand? Why do you think these are or are

not a big deal?

583. Whether or not you believe that our use of the planet could result in melting polar ice caps, you know that changes must be made to keep our planet going. What are some of the keys to our survival in the next 50 years? Is it more important for the government or individuals to take action and why?

584. During a freak cruise ship accident, you were doused with some toxic waste and left for dead in the middle of the ocean. In reality, you were given amazing powers to restore life to the planet and stop bad guys. How do you use these green powers to save the world from pollution?

585. There is no question that there's a conflict between the health of the environment and the health of the economy when it comes to domestic drilling for fossil fuels. Which side do you support the most and why? Would your answer change if foreign sources of oil are no longer available?

586. You couldn't help but fall madly in love with a hippie environmental girl. She was beautiful and was worth all of the meetings and the protests she dragged you to. One day, however, she convinced you to chain yourself to a multi-billion dollar company's front gate and you ended up on all of the cable news channels. Now your family is threatening to cut off your tuition payments. How will you get out of this precarious situation?

587. If you could go back in time and change a few environmental decisions the world has made in the past few hundred years, what would they be and why? If they'd been made differently, how would the world be changed today?

588. Deep, deep within the ocean lies the city of Atlantis, a place that you and your family call home. Recently, the trash and filth dumped into the ocean have begun to seep into your previously pristine land. Against the orders of your parents, you have decided to reveal the plight of your people to the human race. What happens after you set foot on land?

589. The long search for an alternative fuel source has been found on the surface of an asteroid that crash-landed into Earth. Scientists learn to replicate this clean-burning, unlimited fuel and the pollution problems of fossil fuels have been eradicated. What are the next few years like in this much cleaner world?

590. You are a redwood tree in the midst of a slowly decaying forest. You and your family of trees have been declining over the years due to deforestation and pollution. You think back to the times when people revered nature, when you and your fellow trees were planted. What are some of the differences between today and those tree-friendly times?

Magic

591. You've been changed from a human into a talking frog. Yes, you

thought it was a cliché when it happened, too. Now you need to enlist the help of some newly acquired swamp friends to defeat an evil wizard. What happens next in this boggy tale of magical woe?

592. How do you think the prevalence of Harry Potter and similar books have changed the lives of magicians? On one hand, more and more kids are interested in seeing magic. On the other hand, the bar for how amazing that magic needs to be may be set higher than ever. Imagine that you are a famous magician for a room full of Potter fans. How would the party go differently than normal?

593. While doing an oral report on the history of witches, you accidentally take home a book of real spells! When you realize what you have on your hands, you decide to have some fun with it first. What spells do you case and do any of them have a more consequential effect than you originally thought they would?

594. How would your life have been different if you grew up in a world of magic, dragons, and mystical guests? What would your profession be in such a dimension and what would you do during a typical day? Make sure to describe your altered house, clothes, and general appearance.

595. Even though you didn't believe what you were hearing, you decided to spend some leftover allowance on an alleged love potion from an apothecary. For kicks, you try it out on your long-time crush and it works! Since it only took a drop to be effective, how will you use the rest of the bottle?

596. A strange package arrived at your house today, addressed to you from a deceased grandparent. You open it to see a glorified stick and a note that says, "Point this East to find me." Later that night, you comply and a strange blue portal opens up. What do you decide to do next?

597. What do you think it was about the Harry Potter books that made them so successful? After being a sort of taboo subject, magic was now fun for the whole family. What do you think will be the next big literary boom on par with J.K. Rowling's new classics? Will magic be involved and why?

598. If you could have one magic ability, what would it be and why? How would your life change with this newfound power? How would you be different now if you'd had that power your whole life?

599. In some magical role playing and paper/pencil games, certain items, clothing, and weapons are imbued with magical abilities. A helmet might have the power to increase your strength and a pair of boots could magically increase your speed. What would it be like if you could collect magical items like that in real life? Describe your wardrobe and accessories and how each of them magically enhances your abilities. How would the world be different if everyone could collect such mystical relics?

600. An evil and powerful warlock has hypnotized everyone in your town to do his bidding. Only a few were immune from his charms,

including you and your little brother. What is this sorcerer up to and how will you and your brother fight back against the evil? What is it that makes the two of you magic-resistant?

Adulthood

601. When you were a little kid, what did you want to be when you grew up? Has that desire changed? Are you on the path to that dream job? Why or why not?

602. How is life different for the following groups of people: children, teenagers, adults, the elderly? What are some of the challenges each group has to face?

603. What are five words that come to mind when you think of adulthood? Judging by how many positive and negative words you chose, do you think adulthood is a happy or a sad time and why?

604. In your opinion, at what age does someone become an adult? If you're younger than that age, how will your life become different when you hit that magical mark? If you are that age or above, what changed for you by that age and why?

605. How has adulthood changed from when your grandparents became adults and why? Has this change been for the better or the worse and why?

606. What advantages do adults have over children? Conversely, what advantages to children have over adults? Who would win a head-to-head and why?

607. What truly makes a person an adult and why? Do you need all of those qualities to qualify? Why or why not?

608. Kids who live through terrible experiences are said to have to grow up quickly. Would you consider those kids to be adults? Why or why not?

609. Imagine that you went immediately from the age of four to the life of a 40-year-old. What are some things you'd miss out on? Would it be worth it?

610. What are the scariest parts about being an adult? Do you think your parents or grandparents were afraid of those aspects of adulthood as well? Why or why not?

Fairness

611. Think back to a time when your family wouldn't let you do something you really wanted to do. Did you think the decision was fair? Why or why not? Would the situation be different if you were the parent to a child asking the same thing? Why or why not?

612. How do you think you learned your concept of right and wrong, of fair and unfair? How have you applied those concepts in your life?

613. Some things labeled as unfair in the U.S., such as discrimination against women, are considered fair game in other parts of the world. Why do you think the concept of fairness differs so much in some places?

614. What is a situation in which it might be hard to tell what is fair vs. what is unfair? How would you reason out the right decision?

615. You have been transported back 100,000 years in time and put into a sort of prison for being an evil demon. How would you convey that this decision is unfair? Would you be able to get out? Why or why not?

616. What are some of the key differences between a fair society and an unfair society? How would you survive in an unfair society?

617. The judicial system is meant to decide innocence and guilt. Do you think the courts achieve this? Why or why not?

618. Some people think that life is unfair to them, even though others cope with the same circumstances with a lot more optimism. How does attitude relate to fairness? What kind of attitude do you have when something unfair happens to you?

619. Do you think your concept of what's fair and not fair has changed as you've gotten older? Why or why not? How might your opinion of what's fair change in the next five to ten years?

620. Imagine that someone judged you unfairly at first glance. What might they think about you that wasn't true? How would you convince them to fairly judge you going forward?

Creativity

621. Who is the most creative person you know? Why is this person so creative? Do you envy that creativity? Why or why not?

622. Do you enjoy doing creative activities? Why or why not? If you had to choose between standard homework or creative homework, which would you choose and why?

623. Have you ever had a moment of creative inspiration? What did you do with your "Ah Ha" moment and why? How long did the epiphany last?

624. What is your favorite creative medium and why? What would it be like to have a full-time job in that medium and why?

625. Imagine that you could have lunch with any creative person throughout history. Who would you choose and why? What might this creative person inspire you to do?

626. You have magically been granted an unlimited supply of creativity. No matter what you love to do creatively, you can now do it as long as you want without fail or procrastination. How would you use this gift and why?

627. What is the most creative thing you've ever done? Were you proud of it? Why or why not? Do you think you'll ever top it? Why or why not?

628. How do you think people will express their creativity 100 years in

the future? Will they enjoy themselves as much as we do in our creative expression today? Why or why not?

629. How does your creative expression differ from your parents'? How does it differ from your grandparents' creative expression? In what ways is your creativity similar and why?

630. What are some things that cause you to feel less creative? What are the best ways to get rid of those creative roadblocks for you?

Reward and Punishment

631. What do you believe works better: positive reinforcement or negative reinforcement? Which worked better on you with your previous teachers and bosses and why?

632. What is the greatest reward you've ever received? What did you do to deserve this reward and how does it make you feel?

633. What is the harshest punishment you've ever endured? What was so bad about it? Did you deserve the punishment? Why or why not?

634. How would you feel if a close friend or family member was found guilty of a major crime? What would your opinion be of this loved one's punishment and why?

635. After you win high honors for a significant achievement, a secret society has given you the opportunity to decide on your own award. What award will you choose and why?

636. Have you ever punished yourself when you felt bad about something? If so, what did you do and did you deserve it? If not, what do you think might cause you to punish yourself and why?

637. When you were a little kid, would you have gotten in trouble for stealing a cookie from the cookie jar? If so, how would this punishment have taught you never to do it again? If not, how would your parents have handled your theft?

638. What is something you do for someone else on a regular basis that serves as its own reward? Why do some people feel the need to always demand a reward or compensation?

639. Imagine a world in which nobody is ever punished, no matter how terrible the crime. What would happen in such a world over time and why?

640. Which of the following awards would mean the most to you and why: Nobel Prize, Super Bowl Most Valuable Player, Presidential Medal of Freedom, or Sexiest Man or Woman in the World?

Giving and Receiving

641. Which do you enjoy better: giving gifts or receiving them? What do

you think this says about you and why?

642. What is the best gift you've ever received? Why did this present top your list? How did you express your thanks?

643. Everybody has forgotten your birthday! How will your special day change without gifts and a party? How would you remedy this unfortunate situation?

644. Describe the best gift you've ever given. What made it so special and how did you feel when you gave it?

645. Who is someone in your life who is impossible to buy a gift for? Why is it so hard to find this person the item they might like? What are some of your past gift-giving efforts with this person?

646. During a winter secret gift exchange, you've drawn your mortal enemy! What will you get this person in the spirit of the season? How does shopping for your nemesis make you feel about them?

647. Upon opening the biggest gift in the room, you find... that it's the worst gift you've ever received. What is it and why is it so terrible? What will you do to not hurt the gift giver's feelings while making sure you can return it?

648. Which gift-giving and receiving time of year is your favorite and why? What do you think you'll get the next time it comes around? What will you give and why?

649. Your family has decided to forego gifts this winter holiday season. Instead, everyone will get gifts for people in need. How does this make you feel and why?

650. If you could go back in time 10 years to give a gift to yourself, what would it be and why? How would those years be different with the gift in hand?

Power

651. Absolute power is said to corrupt absolutely. Do you feel if you were given enough power that you would be corrupted by it? Why or why not?

652. What parts of your life do you feel you have the most power over and why? What could you do to gain power over the other parts?

653. Who is the most powerful person you know? How did they obtain such power? Do you envy them? Why or why not?

654. After being elected to a local government position, you've been bribed over a million dollars by a special interest group. What happens next?

655. Do you think people in positions of authority can be completely noble and good? Why or why not?

656. Imagine that your best friend has gained a position of power and

it's completely gone to his or her head. What will you do to get your comrade's feet back on the ground? Might it be too late? Why or why not?

657. You've been given the ability to invent your own position of power in the world. What title would you give yourself and what abilities would you have?

658. What would be an example of a person with the least amount of power possible? What would you do if you were that person and why?

659. Describe a time in which you were powerless to stop something from happening. How did it make you feel? What would you do differently if you could to back in time to change things?

660. Imagine you had power over your friends and family members. What would you do with this power and why? How could you use that power to help them?

Attitude

661. When do you think is the worst time to have a bad attitude and why? Which of your friends or family members is the most likely to have that issue and why?

662. When you are feeling cranky, how do you help yourself to find a better attitude? Does this method always work? Why or why not?

663. What are some tough situations in your life that you think you've handled with a good attitude? How were you able to stay positive in such difficult circumstances?

664. How do you handle someone in a bad mood? How do you think you could improve your tactics?

665. Imagine that you needed a big favor from your sibling or friend. How would you try to make sure he or she was in the best mood possible before making the ask? Would you feel bad about buttering him or her up? Why or why not?

666. What does it say about a person when they have a bad attitude during a crisis? Conversely, what does it say about a person if they have a good attitude in tough times? Which side do you fall on and why?

667. Think back to a time when you made a decision that was completely based on your bad mood at the time. What did you do and do you regret the decision? Why or why not?

668. Describe someone in your life who always seems to be in high spirits. Do you think this person is being genuine? Why or why not? If so, what do you think their secret is?

669. The most important job interview of your life is coming up after the worst, most disheartening night of all time. Describe how you spend that morning getting yourself back in a positive mind frame. Will your efforts be successful? Why or why not?

670. How would you describe the attitude of the most successful person you know? How much do you think their attitude has to do with their success?

Help

671. Who is the first person you tend to go to when you need help? What is it that makes this person so reliable?

672. Describe a situation in which you needed a lot of help. Were other people able to help you as much as you required? Why or why not?

673. Imagine that a friend or family member asked you for help one too many times. How would you go about telling them no? How would they react?

674. What would you do if you saw a stranger in need of help? Would your answer change if you were in a dangerous part of town? Why or why not?

675. Do you like helping people? Why or why not? What do you think that says about you?

676. What is the most difficult thing anyone has ever asked you to help them with? Why was it so tough? Did you end up helping them?

677. What is a situation in which it might be embarrassing to ask for help? If you were desperately in need in that area, do you think you'd still ask? Why or why not?

678. What is the first thought that comes to mind when you see a person on the street with a sign that says "Please help"? Are you more likely to help or pass the person by and why?

679. Imagine that you have a great idea for a business but no money to start it up. Who would you first ask for help? What would be your pitch? Do you think you'd successfully get the money? Why or why not?

680. Imagine that you have to help a family member after he or she has undergone a painful medical procedure. What would it be like to wait hand and foot on someone you love? Would you get sick of it? Why or why not?

Competition

681. You've been chosen to compete in the 2020 Olympic Games! What sport are you most likely to compete in? What is it like to be on the world stage competing in front of all those people?

682. While playing a game with your friends, you catch one friend cheating! Do you immediately tell everyone else about the cheater? Why or why not? How do you handle the situation?

683. Have you ever won a competition? If so, what was it like and how did it feel? If not, what competition would you most want to win and why?

684. Where do you think the need for victory comes from and why? Of all the people you know, who has the strongest need to win at all costs and why?

685. In what ways is an academic competition different from an athletic competition? Does one mean more than the other? Why or why not?

686. Do you think you could stand to be more competitive or less competitive and why? How would your life change if you were able to change this aspect of yourself?

687. You have made it to the final round of interviews for the "job of your dreams!" How did you make it so far in the competitive process? What will you need to do to get the job and why?

688. What are some areas outside of athletics, academics, and your career that you have to be competitive in? Who of your friends is the most successful in these areas? Why is he or she such a pro?

689. Do you think competition is a positive thing? Why or why not? In what ways could competition be used in a constructive way in the world?

690. What would you do if you had to compete with a friend over someone you wanted to date? Which would be more important, the friendship or the relationship, and why?

War and Peace

691. While playing a war-based video game, you've been sucked through the screen and into combat! How do you survive in this environment? What would you do to try to escape and why?

692. A war has broken out between two neighboring countries and you've been tasked to come up with a peaceful solution. What do you decide to do to try to patch up relations between the two warring countries? Does it work? Why or why not?

693. There are many terrible consequences of war. What do you think is the worst consequence and why? How would you feel if you suffered such hardship during a war close to home and why?

694. When a conflict arises between you and your peers, are you more likely to fight or to try to resolve things peacefully? What do you think your typical decision says about you?

695. You've been drafted, forcing you to report to duty in less than a week! What do you decide to do and why?

696. What are some of the main reasons that a country's government would decide to go to war? Do you find any of these reasons legitimate? Why or why not?

697. Would a world with peace among all nations be a good place to live? Why or why not? What major changes would need to happen to establish a world that can handle peace?

698. What war would you consider to the most devastating of all time? Would you feel the same way if you were fighting for one of the two sides? Why or why not?

699. Two of your best friends are having a landmark argument. What steps do you take to try to get them to make peace with one another? Is your plan likely to work? Why or why not?

700. Do you think there's a situation in which war is necessary and unavoidable? If so, describe the situation in full, citing as many examples as you can. If not, why might a country's government say that war was inevitable?

Change

701. What would you do if you saw a major change in a friend or loved one and why? Would that same person do the same for you? Why or why not?

702. What is the biggest change you've purposely made in your life? Why did you decide to make this change? Was it for the better? Why or why not?

703. Do you think change is a good thing or a bad thing and why? Will you always feel that why? Why or why not?

704. Sometimes change happens whether we want it to or not. What is the most significant change to happen in your life without your choice? How did this external change impact you internally?

705. You wake up one day to find everything different: you house, your clothes and even yourself! What happens next?

706. When you need to shake things up, what do you usually do to change things and why? How do those changes typically make you feel? Why?

707. If you could change one aspect of your emotions, what would you change and why? Would your friends and family be happy with the change? Why or why not?

708. When people think about changing themselves, they often think about making physical changes. Why are people so concerned about changing their bodies? Do you ever feel the desire to change your body? Why or why not?

709. Do you believe that people can change? Why or why not? If people can change, does that change happen mostly from themselves or other people, and why?

710. Why do you think some people are so afraid of change? Who in your life would you consider to be the most afraid of change and why?

Fulfillment

711. What do you think it means to be fulfilled? What would it take to make you feel fulfilled and why?

712. How would you feel if you achieved all of your life dreams? How long might your fulfillment last and why?

713. What goal in life do you think would leave you feeling the most fulfilled and why? If you did actually achieve it, what would the next step be and why?

714. A series of heartbreaking setbacks have left you feeling completely unfulfilled. How would you dig yourself out of this hole to get back on a positive path?

715. Who is the most fulfilled person you know and why does this person seem so content? Is there anything you can learn from him or her? Why or why not?

716. You are the next big self-help guru and you've risen to fame based on your advice for helping people to feel fulfilled. What is the advice that has helped so many people to be happier, healthier and more fulfilled?

717. Which of the following things do you think are the most important for a deeply fulfilled life and why: money, family, health, love, career success, or happiness?

718. What are some changes you could make to your routine that would make you feel less stressed and more content? How would being more satisfied and happy change your relationships with friends and family?

719. What are some ways the world is built for life fulfillment? What are some ways the world is build against it? Do you think it's easier to be fulfilled or unfulfilled and why?

720. Do you think it was easier for more people to be happy and fulfilled 100 years ago? Why or why not? Will it be easier for people to find fulfillment 100 years in the future? Why or why not?

Miracles

721. Describe a miracle you've experienced or a miracle someone else has told you about. Do you think this event was a true miracle? Why or why not?

722. If you could ask for any miracle to occur in your life, what would it be and why? How would said miracle change things for you?

723. Some people see life as its own miracle. Would you agree with them? Why or why not?

724. Of all the people you know, who is the most deserving of a miracle? What has this person done to earn that miraculous event? How likely do you think it is to happen and why?

725. What are three miracles you think the world could use right now? How many people would those miracles affect and how would they feel after their prayers were answered?

726. People throw around the word miracle all the time, in sports, in the news, and in their everyday lives. How would you best define a miracle? What are a few examples of this more accurately defined miracle?

727. How would the world be different if miracles happened as soon as people asked for them? How might peoples' priorities change in this miracle-heavy world?

728. Would you consider any parts of your life miraculous? If so, what are they and why do they qualify? If not, what miracle would you most want to happen right here and right now, and why?

729. Imagine that you had a terminal illness and you were miraculously cured in a way doctors couldn't explain. How do you think you might live differently after such an experience? Who or what would you thank for your miracle and why?

730. Which of the following concepts would you consider a miracle: love, the start of the universe, flight, or a Hail Mary touchdown pass? Which of these is the most miraculous and why?

CHAPTER 5: MONEY

Money

731. Upon the suggestion of a friend, you have travelled to the far reaches of the world to find out the secrets of money. You came upon a map leading you to the top of a mountain where a bearded, ancient guru would tell you everything you need to know. Once you reach him, you're completely surprised by his advice. What does he suggest and how does employing it change your life?

732. You can't believe your eyes. Your daughter stole a fifty-dollar bill out of your wallet a few weeks ago, planted it in the ground, and now a money tree is actually growing in the backyard. You try to keep it a secret from the neighbors and you're able to harvest the first 1,000 $50 bills before it becomes the talk of the town. Once the story becomes public, how will you protect your precious resource?

733. Who is the wealthiest person that you know personally? How did that person become so affluent and what tips do you think you might be able to glean from his or her success? Has that money contributed positively or negatively to this person's happiness?

734. After having a building inspector check out the foundation of your parents' house, you are surprised to find that there's a tiny gold mine located right underneath the house! The only problem is that your father was raised in the house and he doesn't want anybody messing with it in the slightest. He even put it in his will! Will you try to circumvent him to get the gold or respect his wishes and why?

735. Contrary to popular belief, the wealthiest people don't tend to live extravagantly. In reality, they live well below their means and save up, while those who appear to be the wealthiest are often riddled with debt. How do you think you and your family might be able to live this truer definition of

wealthy? If you came upon a lot of money, would you be prone to spend it quickly like these other seemingly affluent folks?

736. What do you think is a legitimate way that you and your family could become rich? Not the lottery, not some stroke of luck or randomness, but a real way that you could hit the big time tax bracket-wise due to hard work and ingenuity. How would you be able to put this plan into practice?

737. What does it mean to be poor and what does it mean to be rich? How important do you see someone's financial standing as a part of their achievements in this world? Do you think that a person can be poor and still be seen as a success? Why or why not?

738. You and your archaeological team have stumbled upon a seemingly prehistoric society that has absolutely no concept of money. You love how much people work together and how everyone chips in if someone is having a difficult time with health, whether it be mental or physical. Do you decide to make your discovery known, potentially corrupting this society and bringing yourself wealth, or instead, do you decide to give up your life and stay with this tribe? What are the consequences of your decision?

739. In the Cee-Lo Green song "Forget You," the narrator discusses how difficult it his to keep a relationship with the girl he loves because all she cares about is money. Have you ever had a relationship in which you felt like you'd be sunk without sinking more and more dollar bills into gifts and extravagant dates? How would you cope with such a situation if you were madly in love with this moneygrubber?

740. A self-made millionaire has come up to you requesting that you write his biography. If the book is successful at demonstrating his true message of peace and love to the world, he will give you his entire fortune. How do you successfully convey his thoughts in your book and are you able to convince him to give you all his money? What happens after publication?

Debt

741. There are many different types of debt. When the word comes to mind, what type of debt do you think of and why?

742. When you are in someone's debt, how does it make you feel? How would it feel if you were able to wipe your debts clean with this person and why?

743. Your best friend owes you a lot of money and he or she is way behind on the payments. How do you handle this situation? Why do you choose to handle it that way?

744. One of your family members is in debt to a group of shady individuals. How did your loved one get in this situation? Would you be willing to help him or her out? Why or why not?

745. Has someone every done something for you and you told them they did not need to return the favor? How did it feel giving out a free favor and why?

746. After a strange turn of events, you've saved a fierce warrior's life. This warrior now wants to follow you around and protect you for the rest of time. In what ways will the warrior protect you? Is he or she helpful or annoying, and why?

747. You are deep in financial debt and you have to get rid of everything. Your phone, your computer, your house and everything in between. How might it feel to start over at zero because of your large debts? What would you have to do to pay it all off and why?

748. Who in your life would least like to be in debt to and why? If you did owe this person something, how would you have to repay it?

749. During a dinner conversation, your parents have told you that they're in deep debt and need your help. How would you assist them out of this problem? What are some ways you might get them to help themselves?

750. Why do people buy so much stuff when they can't afford it? Is it more important to have an extravagant lifestyle for a few years or a sensible and sustainable life for decades and why?

The Economy

751. Whatever you believe has led to a rough economy in the present, it seems almost a given that it's the case of a few valuing their own needs over the needs of the masses. What do you think causes a person to make such an immoral set of decisions? Write a bit from that person's perspective in defending him or herself.

752. One of the most talked about issues in the economy in the last few months is the plight of the 99 percent. What do you think are the main demands of the 99 percent movement and do you think those causes have been expressed well? What would be the best way for the 99 percent to get what it wants?

753. Imagine what your life would be like if you were in the top one percent of income in your country. What opinions would you have about United States economic policy? How would this different from your current views and why? Do you think you'd exert influence on policymakers due to your large accounts?

754. Take away the media and politicians and strip it down to its core: what is the cause of this and past recessions? Do you think that these recessions could have been avoided or were they inevitable and why? What law or action could prevent future recessions from happening and why?

755. Ayn Rand, a controversial figure in economy, philosophy and literature, referred to capitalism as the only moral system of government.

What do you think Rand, who grew up in an oppressive communist regime, meant by this assessment? How closely does your opinion of capitalism line up with Rand's and why?

756. It seems like in the grand scheme of things, a regular person can't do much to improve the economy in general. What do you think are the best actions an average Joe or Jane can do to aid the economy? How would the economy be affected if millions of people followed those actions?

757. There have been times during this country's existence where it seemed like a much greater percentage of people were living affluently. What would it be like to live in one of those times and to have a much higher chance of being wealthy? How would your life differ from its current economic state?

758. You have been given a difficult choice by a wizard from another realm. You can bring prosperity back to the country you love, the people you love, and future generations. In return, you must live out the rest of your days as a penniless beggar. What do you decide and why? Describe the aftermath of your decision.

759. One current issue with the economy is that many jobs have been outsourced to countries where labor is cheaper. A recent development is the knowledge that this labor is kept cheap through horrible conditions. What do you think is the solution to the outsourcing problem, keeping in mind that simply bringing all the jobs to the U.S. would double or triple the cost of many goods?

760. How does the look of a typical affluent person compare with the look of a poor person? How do their characters tend to compare? Why is it that money tends to change people character-wise, whether they have it or don't?

Technology

761. What do you think is the most important piece of technology that has been created in your lifetime and why?

762. Ever since the iPhone was launched, people have been obsessed with apps. What is your favorite app and why?

763. If you could create your own app, what would it be and why? Would the app make you rich and famous? Why or why not?

764. Fifty years ago people thought that people would be using flying cars and hovercrafts by now. What technologies to you anticipate that we will have fifty years from now? Do you think we'll live up to those expectations? Why or why not?

765. Do you enjoy playing video games? Why or why not? Why are video games so popular?

766. What technology gets on your nerves? Why does this technology

bother you so much? How do you deal with this feeling in your everyday life?

767. Facebook, Twitter, and other social media sites have in many ways brought people closer together and in other ways driven people further apart more than ever. Does social media really bring people together? Why or why not?

768. Imagine that you've gotten into an argument with someone over a Facebook status or a Tweet. Describe the argument. Is there a point to this online bickering? Why or why not?

769. Do you find enjoyment from finding out the ordinary events from people's days on Facebook and Twitter? Why or why not? Do you think it's important to post about the little things? Why or why not?

770. If we lost all of our technologies overnight, how would we cope as a society? How would you handle yourself and why?

Shopping

771. You have been given an unlimited Visa credit card as part of a promotion, enabling you to purchase everything and anything you want from your favorite mall. The catch is that you only have three hours and it all needs to fit into your car. What is your purchasing strategy, what do you buy, and what's the grand purchase total of everything you get?

772. While some are brave enough to go to the store on Christmas Eve and Black Friday, others are content to wait until the quieter, more gentle shopping times. Imagine that you have been required to wait in line and find a precious item during one of these wild shopping events. What must you do to successfully get what you came for?

773. During very material-based holidays like Christmas and birthdays, there are many people who can't afford to get the gifts they want. Create a story in which you and your family set out on a quest to provide the presents that a deserving family should receive during such a holiday. What do you do and what makes this family particularly deserving?

774. Do you fit the typical gender stereotype of a guy who hates shopping and a gal who wants nothing more than to max out a credit card? Why or why not? How do you think those stereotypes came about and how much water do those theories hold with your friends and relatives? How high does shopping rank in your top 100 things to do and why?

775. While shopping typically refers to smaller purchases like groceries and batteries, some shopping such as car shopping, engagement ring shopping, and house shopping can lead to a major dent in the wallet. Write a story about a real or made up shopping experience with one of those big life choices and how successful you were with your purchase. How did you come up with the money and was it well spent?

776. Shopping with your parents when you're a kid is a much different experience from when you're first out shopping on your own. What are some of the lessons you learned from your first few solo shopping trips? Did these shortcomings make you appreciate more what your parents had to do when they lugged you around for clothes, food, and accessories? Why or why not?

777. Have you ever had to go into a less than reputable store to purchase an item? What was the most run-down, frightening shopping experience you've ever engaged in and what happened that made it stick out so much in your mind?

778. Imagine that you have loaded up your cart full of items, only to have all of your cards declined at the checkout counter. Not only that, but the cards have come up stolen and now you're sitting back in the security office trying to explain yourself! What happens next in this case of shopping mistaken identity?

779. Have you ever accidentally purchased a major lemon when it came to a car, electronics, or another used shopping experience? How did you go about dealing with this piece of junk and were you ever able to get your money back? Were you tempted to legally get back at the person selling it? Why or why not?

780. Now that so much shopping occurs online, the shopping experience has been changed forever! What are some of the positive and negative aspects of this online shift? Do you enjoy online or in person shopping better? Is it worth the danger of the easiest impulse buying ever created?

Advertising

781. You see a commercial that advertises your favorite food. What is the food and what about the commercial attracts your attention?

782. You are a highly paid advertising executive and one of your clients wants to take her business to a different company. What kind of product does your client sell and what do you do to make her stay?

783. If you could create a new form of advertising, what would it be and why? What do you think is the best way to catch people's attention in advertising and why?

784. You get a job as a casting agent for a company that makes commercials! What is your first commercial about and who is in your dream cast to play the leading men and ladies?

785. You get a contract from the tastiest burger joint in town to reinvent its image for customers. Describe what the new logo would look like. What kind of new customers would the logo bring in and why?

786. Think about a song you've heard online or on the radio advertising for a specific product. Did the song make you want to buy it? Why or why not?

787. Your boss is going to fire you unless you design the best ad campaign in the world to attract people's attention! What will you do to stand out as unique? Will your efforts be enough to save your job? Why or why not?

788. It's Super Bowl Sunday, the best day of the year for the funniest commercials! What is your favorite Super Bowl commercial of all time and why? What are the most important aspects of a successful Super Bowl commercial?

789. You are asked to lead an ad campaign for a product that you do not support. Will you go ahead with the campaign despite your beliefs? Why or why not?

790. If you had to create the worst commercial in the world, what ideas would you put into it? What are some of the bad commercials you've seen that have inspired you to create such a terrible ad?

CHAPTER 6: LOVE AND ENTERTAINMENT

Dating

791. What is something that you'd never bring up on a first date? Why would that subject be so taboo?

792. It's been said that first impressions are everything. How would you want a person describe you after a first date? Do you think you'd be able to pull that off? Why or why not?

793. Describe the most awkward date you've ever been on. What made it so memorably awkward? Did you still go on another date with this person and why? If you've never been on a date, make up a story of the most awkward date imaginable.

794. What might be some of the positives and negatives of being in a long-term dating relationship with someone? Do the benefits outweigh the detriments? Why or why not?

795. How do people in a dating relationship behave differently from single people? Would you behave in the same way if you were in a relationship? Why or why not?

796. What would you say is the point of dating: having fun, meeting someone you might marry, or something completely different? Why do you feel that way?

797. After five dates, your girlfriend or boyfriend wants you to meet the parents! How will you prepare for this encounter? Do you think it'll go well? Why or why not?

798. Breaking up is hard to do, but it's a part of dating. Do you think it's possible to have a friendly break-up with someone you've dated? Why or why not?

799. What are five things you can learn from dating? How might you be able to apply these learnings to other parts of your life?

800. You knock on your door to find a talking baby with a bow and arrow. It's Cupid and he's giving you a chance to have your dream date with your #1 crush. What will your dream date with this person consist of and why? How would this date make you feel?

Valentine's Day

801. What is the most memorable Valentine's Day you've ever experienced? Describe the day from beginning to end, including what you felt, what you did, and who you were with. Remember, "memorable" does not mean it was necessarily good or bad, it just means that it is deeply imbedded in your mind!

802. You have decided to prove your love with an amazing display of affection and gifts during a Valentine's Day celebration with your significant other. What do you get your love for the holiday and what do you have planned out to sweep your paramour off his or her feet?

803. If you could create a card for Valentine's Day, what would it say and why? What kind of demographic do you think would like it the most? Would you ever give this card to someone you care about in particular and why or why not?

804. The early origins of Valentine's Day had nothing to do with romantic love and the holiday didn't change to include love until the times of Geoffrey Chaucer and courtly love. Imagine that you had the ability to change what multiple holidays actually celebrated. What holidays would you change and why? How would their celebrations change?

805. With your love out of town for Valentine's Day, you have been tasked with cheering up your single friends during the holiday. What do you do to pep up those who are unlucky in love and how do these lonely folks react to you in your attempt to bring independent cheer?

806. In what feels like a plot out of a bad movie, you have been visited by apparitions of all your past partners, who are trying to collectively teach you a lesson about love. Why have they come now and what is the lesson they might want to instruct you in? Will you learn it or continue to go on about love as you always had?

807. As an arrow goes whizzing by your face, you drive to the ground and hear what seems like a toddler laughing. It's Cupid! Not only is this baby of love real, but he wants to grab a bite to eat with you to talk about love. What do you and Cupid talk about and what is he like in real life?

808. You have been tasked with creating the ultimate Valentine's Day playlist for a big holiday dance at a local group you belong to. What are some of the biggest hits about love you add to the list? What are the reactions like to your loving music selection?

809. Some guys and girls simply don't have a clue when it comes to

Valentine's Day. What are some of the worst gifts you've ever heard being exchanged on this pink and red holiday? Can you think of any gifts that would be even worse? What reactions might these gifts provoke?

810. How would you explain Valentine's Day to an immigrant from another country who'd never before experienced it? What aspects of the holiday might this person think quaint, strange, or downright ridiculous?

Weddings

811. Imagine that you could create a new wedding tradition that would catch on like wildfire. What would this new tradition be and why would it be so popular?

812. What do you think is the most boring part of a wedding? What are three ways that you could spice it up? Would everybody at the wedding enjoy your changes?

813. You are the best man or the maid of honor at your best friend's wedding. A few minutes before the ceremony starts, your friend asks if he or she should go through with it. What happens next?

814. What is the most memorable wedding you've ever attended? What parts do you remember most clearly and why? If you've never been to a wedding, make up a story about the wedding of two close friends.

815. Describe your ideal wedding from the start of the ceremony to the end of the reception getaway. What parts would you want to make traditional and what parts would be unique? Would everyone enjoy it as much as you? Why or why not?

816. Do you think that a great wedding is important for a successful marriage? Why or why not?

817. Write the worst wedding vows you can think of. What would you think if you heard these vows spoken during a ceremony and why?

818. Weddings can cost tens or hundreds of thousands of dollars, even though they only last a single day. Do you think that kind of expenditure is worth it? Why or why not? Would you feel differently if you didn't have to pay for it? Why or why not?

819. Do you think you'd have what it takes to be a wedding planner? Why or why not? What might be the toughest part for you if you had to plan a wedding alone?

820. You've been invited to a wedding of a friend you barely know. The wedding is a complete disaster. What goes wrong and how do you feel while watching it? Would you consider trying to step in and help? Why or why not?

Fairy Tales

821. Fairy tale characters have captured the hearts of readers for ages. If you could meet one fairy tale character, who would it be and why? How would the character react to meeting a real, live person and why?

822. Your magical fairy godmother has arrived to help you succeed in your life! In what ways does she try to help you change your life, and why do you deserve the help?

823. If you could create your own fairy tale land, what would it look like? Describe the land and its inhabitants in full. Why did you choose to create this place?

824. In most fairy tales the good people triumph and bad people lose. What if a fairy tale did not work out that way? Think of a well-known fairy tale, or a fairy tale of your own creation, and change it so that the villain wins in the end. How does this affect the other people in the story after the fairy tale ends in the hero's defeat?

825. What is your favorite fairy tale and why? Imagine what it would be like to be a character in that particular tale. How would your influence change the nature of the story?

826. Most fairy tales happen in ancient times or in far off lands. Create a modern day fairy tale set around the area where you currently live or where you once lived. What would happen in the story and how might you play a part?

827. In the story of Pinocchio, a cricket represents the main character's conscience. If your conscience could take a physical form, what would it look like and why? How would having this tangible conscience change how you live your everyday life?

828. In fairy tales, villains create obstacles for the heroes to overcome. In your life, who are some people who create your obstacles? What are the obstacles and how do you overcome them?

829. Fairy tale characters have stepped out of the pages of your books and are invading your life! Describe and name these intruding characters. Do you try to make them go back to where they came from? Why or why not?

830. Name one fairy tale character you identify with and why you feel the two of you are similar. Would you do anything different from the character if you were in his or her magical world? Why or why not?

Movies

831. What is your guilty pleasure movie? What is it about this movie that makes you embarrassed to share your love for it with others?

832. What is your top movie to watch when you're feeling down in the

dumps? Why does this movie make you feel better?

833. After a nationwide casting search, you've been chosen to star in a new movie! What's the movie's title and plot? What kind of character do you play? Is it a hit? Why or why not?

834. How has your favorite movie changed over the years? Why do you think your preference has developed the way it has? How do you think your movie love will change going forward?

835. You and all your friends have been excited for a certain movie for an entire year. When you all get to the theater on opening night, it's terrible! How would you react to this disappointing event and why?

836. Which movie genre do you enjoy the most and why? How does your genre taste differ from that of your family members? Is there a kind of movie you can all enjoy together? Why or why not?

837. Do you think the craziest story of your life could work in a movie? Why or why not? If so, who would play you and why?

838. What makes a movie a "good" movie? Does a movie have to be good to be enjoyable? Why or why not?

839. Why do you think movie stars are so famous? Would you be nervous if you had a chance to meet a movie star? Why or why not?

840. What is it about seeing a movie in a theater that is such a great experience for people? Do you think it's worth the extra money? Why or why not?

Photos

841. Describe the feelings that occur when you look through an old family photo album. Have those feelings changed as you've gotten older? Why or why not?

842. Photography is becoming more and more digital, doing away with the concept of the tangible photograph. Do you think this is a positive trend? Why or why not?

843. Imagine looking at a photo of you from five years ago. What would you say has changed about you in that time? What has stayed the same? Are you happy with the changes? Why or why not?

844. What are the events in your life you feel require the most pictures and why? Do you think you have your photo-taking priorities straight? Why or why not?

845. While rummaging through a junk drawer, you find an old picture of yourself. It starts talking to you! What does the picture say and how do you respond? What happens next?

846. What would you say is your most embarrassing photo? Would you want to hide this picture from others or share it and why?

847. Some people hate being photographed, while others can't get

enough of it. Why might some people never want to get their photos taken? In which category do you fall and why?

848. While looking at a picture of a grandparent at the same age as you, you begin to enter the photo itself! Would you and your much younger grandparent get along? What would you do to try to get out of the photo?

849. Now almost every cell phone has a camera on it. It has led to thousands of Facebook photos, Instagrams, Snapchats and more. How often do you take advantage of this technology? Would you rather photograph something awesome or just experience it once? Why?

850. If you could choose a day from your life to go back and document with a camera, what day would it be and why? What would you do with those pictures and why?

Television

851. If you're like most people, you've probably watched hundreds if not thousands of different television programs in your lifetime. Which would you say is the program that affected you the most and why? What effect do you believe the program may have had on others?

852. Come up with a pitch for your ideal television show. What genre is your show and who should star in it? Is it a drama, comedy or something else entirely? Write it out as if you'll be meeting with the executive of your favorite network tomorrow.

853. You have just gotten a part on a highly ranked network television show and the viewers have loved your character so much that you've been promoted to a series regular! What do you think it's like going into work each day to record your acting to be beamed into the homes of millions? Is it more difficult or easier than most people think and why?

854. Despite our best efforts, from time to time we watch a television show and afterwards, we wish we had that half hour, hour, or entire season's worth of time back. What are three shows that fit that category for you? Why did you feel watching them was a waste of time and how would you have personally fixed the shows?

855. Back in the day, television only had a few broadcast channels that nearly everybody in the world sat down to watch. Currently, with hundreds of choices, many loyal network television viewers have moved on to other channels from time to time. How do you think the television landscape will change in the next 50 years and why?

856. One can't help but be enticed by the wild participants in the phenomenon known as reality television. What is your opinion of this genre? Do you think that you would make a decent reality show participant? What show would you be in and why?

857. While you can still currently watch "Wheel of Fortune" and

"Jeopardy" every weeknight, game shows seem to have been mostly pushed to the side in this day and age. What would your idea be for a new game show that could bring the viewers back? Which network would it be on and why?

858. Imagine that as part of an exchange program, you and your family have taken in a child from a remote area where television has never even been heard of. How would you explain this box of shows and entertainment to this student? Are you concerned that he might become extremely addicted after being TV-free for so long?

859. Who are you TV crushes past and present? Why do you have such an attraction to them and how do you think you would act if you ever had a chance to meet them? What if you had a chance to go on a date with them?

860. With giant television screens of more than 70 inches available for homes and 3D televisions making a move into homes, what would you consider the best television viewing experience? Could you be satisfied watching television on your portable devices or computer? What kind of foods, clothes, and other accessories are a TV-watching must?

Desserts

861. What is a dessert that you might reserve for a special occasion? When would you treat yourself to that dessert and why? Do you think you'd like it as much if you had it daily? Why or why not?

862. What is a situation in which you think you deserve a dessert? Does this situation occur everyday? Why or why not?

863. What would you be willing to do to get your favorite dessert right this second? What do you think that says about you?

864. You've been appointed as a pastry chef to the Queen of England! What is the first dessert you'd make to show her how good you are? Would she be convinced of your pastry prowess? Why or why not?

865. How would your life change if desserts were no longer available? What other ways might you find to treat yourself unrelated to sweets?

866. You're extremely excited about your birthday party, until you see that your family didn't buy you a cake. Instead, they bought you the worst dessert on the planet. What is the dessert and how does it make you feel on your birthday? Is there a nice way to tell them you'd like something different? Why or why not?

867. Describe a night out with your loved ones at a local ice cream shop. What flavors would everybody be most likely to get? What would your flavor choice say about you and why?

868. Imagine a world where everything was made out of chocolate. How would the world be different from our world? What things would change in your day-to-day life and why?

869. Which would you enjoy more and why: creating your own dessert from scratch in the kitchen or having someone else make you a delicious dessert? If you had to make your own dessert, what would you choose to create and why?

870. How many meals in a row do you think you could replace with dessert until you got sick? What would some of your sweet meals consist of and why?

Basketball

871. You wake up one day to find that you barely fit into your own bed. As you shake the cobwebs loose and glance into the mirror, you've grown to over seven feet tall. It doesn't take long for a local basketball coach to recruit you for a game, during which you dunk with ease. How does your newfound height and basketball prowess affect your life and why?

872. While some love the high-flying antics of the massive professional players of the NBA, others are much more intrigued by the rivalries and passionate fan bases of the NCAA. Which league would you rather watch if you were given a chance? Which would you be more likely to attend and why?

873. You are a diehard basketball fan. You've just met your soul mate, who is also a diehard basketball fan. Here's the problem: you love the opposite teams in a bitter rivalry going back for decades. How does this opposition affect your relationship? How do you handle watching games between your two teams?

874. One of the things that sets basketball fans apart from other fans is how raucous the crowd can be in a much smaller indoor stadium than football or baseball. Describe the wildest game you've ever attended or seen on television and put yourself in the middle of the action. Did you or did you not enjoy the experience and why?

875. This year, one of the biggest stories in professional basketball is that they might not play professional basketball due to a labor disagreement. If you sat down with one of the major representatives of the player's union, what would you say to them about the game of basketball ? What would his or her response be?

876. If you could be a professional basketball star, what position would you play and why? Would you be more of a no-look passing point guard or a take it to the hole power forward? Would you be the high-flying dunker or the ridiculously tall rebounder? Explain your choice and why you chose it and describe a typical game for yourself.

877. In the list of most exhilarating moments in all of basketball, an expertly choreographed dunk has to be near the top. Last year, Blake Griffin jumped over a car. If you were a dunking champion, what would

you do to top such a momentous feat? How would fans react?

878. You and your team are in the huddle and the coach has drawn up the final play. There are only five seconds remaining, the team is down by two, and the final three-point shot is going to go to you! Describe the play from beginning to end and how successful your final shot is. What is the aftermath of this attempt at buzzer-beating heroism?

879. Down on your luck, you finally take up the offer that a friend of yours with the local basketball team has been making to you for years. You suit up and you wonder, will you truly be able to live down your job wiping down the sweat on the basketball court? Describe the highlights from your first few games and whether or not you enjoy being so close to the action.

880. Which do you find more impressive: the tricks and skills displayed by a touring team like the Harlem Globetrotters or the strength and physical abilities displayed by a professional team on a day-to-day basis? Which team would you rather be a part of?

On The Road

881. Where have you always wanted to travel and why? What's the first thing you would do when you got there?

882. Are you the kind of person who seeks the open road or would you rather stay in one place? Why do you think you developed this preference?

883. Imagine your ideal road trip. Who would you take with you and where would you be traveling? Describe a one-hour stretch of driving in the middle of nowhere.

884. During a road trip in an unfamiliar place, one of your friends has been kidnapped! What is the first thing you do to try to get your friend back? How does the situation get resolved?

885. What is your favorite memory from a road trip with your family? Would the rest of your family enjoy looking back on that memory as much as you? Why or why not?

886. How do you feel when you drive? How would that feeling change in the following scenarios: during a long stretch of empty highway, stuck in traffic, on a road along the coast at sunrise.

887. Name three places you would never want to drive to in all your life. Create a story about being forced to travel to one of them. How would you survive your ordeal?

888. How would your life be different if you had a driving job as a truck or taxicab driver? What would these professions teach you and why?

889. You have won a $25,000 contest with a major car company for a solo road trip tour of America! Which places will you travel to and why? Will you miss your friends and family while you're gone? Why or why not?

890. Would you rather be the driver or the passenger? Does that say

anything about you? Why or why not?

Games

891. Do you think that competition during games brings people together or drives them apart and why? Which outcome would be more likely if your family were to play a game together?

892. Imagine that you've been given a contract to create your own game. With unlimited resources at your disposal, what kind of game will you create and why? What would your friends think about the game and why?

893. Would you rather play a game that involves strategy or random chance and why? What do you think that choice says about you?

894. Describe a person in your life who seems to play games with other people. How do you interact with this person? Why do you think this person acts the way they act?

895. What is the best game playing experience you've ever had? What did you play, who was there, and why was it so enjoyable?

896. If you were stuck at home during a power outage, what electricity-free game would you most want to play and why? Would you enjoy it more than TV and the internet? Why or why not?

897. Do you find any games too difficult to be any fun? If so, what game is too hard to be entertaining and why? If not, create an idea for a game that would be too tough for you and your friends to play.

898. Do you think that life is a game? Why or why not? Why do you think some people have more fun than others in their day-to-day lives?

899. You are stuck playing the game you hate the most with the relatives you despise. What is the game and how do you pass the hours during this dreadful encounter?

900. Have you ever tried to play a game with other people to try to get what you wanted? If so, what did you do and what was the outcome? If not, imagine and describe a situation that might cause you to be a game player.

CHAPTER 7: MIXED BAG

Fire

901. In an ancient myth, fire was given to us by the god Prometheus, which he later paid for dearly for all of eternity. How do you think it really went down? Create your own human origin story for fire and how we learned to control it.

902. Pyromaniacs are people obsessed with the creation and control of fire. How do you think such a person develops such a compulsion related to fire and how can he or she best keep it under control? How would your life be different if you were a pyromaniac?

903. You have been given free juggling lessons as part of a promotion through your school. The final lesson is an attempt to juggle flaming torches. Do you go ahead with it and show your friends your skills or do you shy away for fear of getting burned? Why do you choose that option?

904. Your parents may have told you never to play with matches, but that doesn't mean you always listened. Write a story about how you once played with fire, nearly got in trouble and extinguished the problem before it got out of hand. After such an incident, how would you handle fire safety with your kids?

905. You wake up to find that smoke is lining the top of your room and the doorknob feels too hot to open. You know that you've got to get out or at least get help. How do you survive this house fire? What will you keep in your room in the future to keep yourself safe if it happens again?

906. You and your friends are sitting around a fire during a camping trip. How do you take advantage of it? Do you roast weenies, tell ghost stories, make s'mores, do a war dance, or all of the above? Describe your campfire evening from beginning to end.

907. Firefighters are tough, trained individuals who are willing to risk

their lives to protect the people around them. What do you think it would be like to be a firefighter as a full-time job? How would it change your life and the lives of people around you?

908. Fire can be used to create amazing construction projects and works of art. It can also consume property and lay waste to a life in a heartbeat. What kind of personal relationship do you have with fire? Are you mostly afraid of it or do you feel in control and why?

909. Sometimes, fire can become harmful and can lead to some serious burns. Do you know anyone who has sustained major burns from fire? How have those reminders of the event changed their lives? How would such a scarring reminder change your life?

910. One of the greatest signs of reverence is to have an immortal flame outside of your grave. What do you think you'd have to do in your life to deserve an immortal flame? How would your family feel if you achieved that end result?

Weather

911. You and your family live in an extremely dry and warm part of the world. Due to this confluence of conditions, you occasionally need to pick up and go because of brushfires. What would it be like having to constantly be aware of such a potential dangerous and uprooting event?

912. You look outside and it appears as if the grass is greener than it's ever been. You've never before experienced weather that was so perfect and you want to take complete advantage of it. How do you utilize this beautiful day from beginning to end and why?

913. You ignored the warnings to evacuate, instead spending your time boarding up and sealing every square inch of your generations-old family home. You knew there was a good change the house could get swept away in this historic storm, but you refuse to go down without a fight. As the flood waters rise, what do you do to keep yourself and your house still standing?

914. This is what you wore the rubber boots for. You felt a strange sensation as the electricity from the lighting bolt went coursing through your body. Fortunately, you were prepared. How has having lighting pass through your body changed your life? Will you live your life differently after having been so close to death?

915. You have to pull over as your passengers whine about stopping. Before you and your family took a trip to England, you heard it could be foggy, but you never realized it'd be like this. As you sit in the car and wait for it to clear up, what do you and your family chat about? How long until you brave the perilous monster fog again?

916. How has the concept of snow and ice changed for you as you've

gotten older? Do you miss playing with snowballs and making snowmen? Have you had to brave the icy roads to get to work? How has your life changed as the snow remained the same?

917. While watching your favorite TV show with your friends, the thunderstorm outside causes the power to go out. After finding a flashlight and some candles, how do you all salvage the evening together? Which was more fun, watching the show or having a powerlessly good time together and why?

918. If you had to choose between living somewhere incredibly warm or tooth-chatteringly cold, which would you pick and why? How would you adapt to life in this new weather environment? What would your typical day be like?

919. You walk outside to see if it's raining, and when you hold out your palm a frog falls right into it. Suddenly, hundreds of frogs crash down to Earth and you go back inside. What has caused this strange meteorological event? How will you go about dealing with all these dang frogs?

920. Imagine that you lived the life of a storm chaser in order to find out more about tornados for the sake of science. What dangers would you face and how close to death would you come? What would actually cause you to take up such a dangerous trade?

Air Travel

921. Both the pilot and the co-pilot of your passenger plane have become completely ill and nobody on board knows the first thing about flying. You've drawn the short straw and you have been forced to speak with the radio operator to get your plane to the ground safely. What happens next and do you end up getting to the ground safely and soundly?

922. Describe your most uncomfortable and unfortunate flying experience. Make sure to describe the seating arrangements, the food, your internal monologue and digestion, and anything else that may have been disagreeing with you during your journey. Is there anything you could have done to improve the awful flight? Why or why not?

923. While sitting in the wing row of the airplane a flash of lighting has caused you to see it. No, not a gremlin on the wing, but something much more frightening. What do you see and how do you convince the rest of the passengers to believe you and not think you're crazy?

924. What are five things that you think would make air travel more comfortable and entertaining? Explain how each one of them would add to the flying experience. Do you think such improvements to airplanes would ever be possible or that they'd add too much to the airline's bottom line?

925. A friend of yours has won millions of frequent flyer miles to give to his favorite people in the world, and you've made the cut. Now you have

free flights anywhere a plane can get you for the rest of your life. What places in the world will you travel to that you'd never even dreamed of visiting and why? How will you properly thank your friend?

926. Imagine that you have decided to visit a friend who lives in the middle of nowhere in a third-world country. You don't realize at the time, but the only way to get there is by taking a rickety old airplane that looks like it was last inspected by the Wright brothers. Describe your experience from takeoff to landing. Is visiting your friend worth risking such a flight again?

927. Have you ever taken a helicopter tour of a city or island? If so, write about your experience about seeing the world from a much different view. If not, create a story in which you get to view your favorite city in the world from the view of an extremely safe and secure copter.

928. Within the last decade, several airlines have filed for bankruptcy despite millions of passengers every day paying boatloads to quickly get from point A to point B. How could this have happened? Try to explain how a major airline could possibly have that much debt when making money hand over fist every day of the year. If you ran an airline, how would you solve the problems?

929. Imagine that you have decided to launch a second career as a flight attendant. What is your life like having to travel back and forth from city to city dozens of times in a single week? Do you ever use this ability to visit new and unusual places? What are the customers like and are they a highlight or a lowlight of the job?

930. What is your typical way to pass the time on an extremely long flight? Describe the way you spend your time from beginning to end. Do you think you could be more productive or entertained by planning your itinerary ahead of time? Why or why not?

Yearbooks

931. What was the nicest yearbook message you ever received? Who wrote it? Did it mean more to you when it was written or does it mean more in the present and why?

932. From what year was your favorite yearbook picture and why? How would you describe what might have been going on in your mind while it was taken?

933. You have travelled back in time and become yearbook editor for a key year of middle or high school. Would you be inclined to put in more pictures of yourself or fewer pictures of yourself and why?

934. When looking through an old yearbook, how many pictures would you see of people with whom you are no longer friends? What are some of the reasons you didn't stay friends with these people? If you had the chance

to reconnect, would you? Why or why not?

935. Were you featured in a lot of pictures in your yearbooks? If so, what were you doing in those pictures? If not, what would you have been doing if you were more prominent and why?

936. If you could re-live one yearbook-esque memory, what would it be and why? How would re-living that memory make you feel and why?

937. If you could visit your favorite teacher or school faculty member featured in one of your yearbooks, what would you say to this person and why? Would this person be proud of you? Why or why not?

938. If you were to construct a yearbook of your life right now, what would it look like? Who would be in this yearbook? What moments would you include from the past year?

939. "Have a great summer" is one of the all-time standard yearbook signatures. Did you ever write something like that in a friend's yearbook? What are some other non-thoughtful things you might have written in the yearbooks of people you didn't know very well?

940. One of your yearbooks has fallen out of your shelf, almost magically opening to a page you've never seen before. It's a note from a person you haven't seen in years. What does this secret note say? Do you do anything about it? Why or why not?

Shapes

941. If you could redesign every item, building, and landmark on Earth to be the same shape, what shape would you choose and why? What do you think your choice says about you?

942. You get trapped in a crazy maze full of strange shape-filled rooms. Describe the maze in its entirety: its hallways, hidden alcoves, and other creepy features. Are you able to get out of this wacky maze?

943. How do you think the world would be different if suddenly every square item turned into a circle? How would you be personally affected?

944. If shapes had a specific taste, smell, and feel, how would the world change? How would you describe a rectangle in this new world using your five senses?

945. What is your favorite shape and why? How do you think you came to love this shape so much?

946. The world is round, but people once thought that it was flat. What do you think Earth would be like if the world had turned out to be flat instead of round?

947. What shape do you find to be the most functional in our society and why?

948. What would our world be like if all rooms were shaped like three-dimensional triangles instead of rectangles and cubes? How would you

adjust to a three-walled world?

949. In your childhood, did you find the act of stacking blocks satisfying or boring? Describe the experience in full and why playing with blocks may have been an important part of childhood.

950. Picture the street you live on. What are some of the shapes you see as you walk down the block? Which shape is the most prevalent? Why do you think that is?

Colors

951. You get trapped in a kaleidoscope, a toy tube with a constantly changing set of patterns and colors. Describe what you see. How do you go about getting out of the kaleidoscope?

952. You are building your dream house! What color paint do you pick for each room? Why did you match up those colors with those rooms?

953. Some colors are just disgusting. What is a color that you absolutely hate? What about this color makes you despise it so much?

954. If you could pick a color to describe each of your immediate family members, what colors would you pick and why? What would your family members think of the colors that you picked for them?

955. Chameleons have the ability to change their color to match the background behind them. If you had this adaptation, what situations you use it in and why?

956. What color makes you the most emotional and why?

957. After a science experiment gone wrong, the world has suddenly become black and white with no colors in between! What colors do you miss the most and why? How do you adapt to living in a black-and-white world?

958. If you could change the colors of the American flag, what colors would you choose and why? What about those colors better represents America than red, white, and blue?

959. If you could hear colors instead of seeing them, what would they sound like and why? Imagine your favorite color and describe the sound that it makes.

960. If happiness and sadness had colors, what would they be and why? Analyze a few other emotions, and decide what color best fits each emotion and why.

Moving

961. It was hard to break up with your high school love when your parents had to move, but you've moved on and started over in love with someone new. Coincidentally, your old love's parents had to move too, and

to the same new place! Now you're stuck in an old-fashioned love triangle! What happens next in this tough love situation?

962. Have you ever had to move from a place you really, truly loved? What is it you appreciated so much about that location and what did you miss the most about leaving? What advantages were there in your new home?

963. It's moving day and all of your friends will be there to help. Then again, moving day is never that simple. A few hours later, everything that could go wrong did go wrong and as you pick up a waterlogged box from the gutter, you wonder what happened. What went down and how did your stuff end up in a gutter?

964. Imagine what it'd be like if you had to move permanently to another country. How would you go about finding a place, transporting your stuff, and saying goodbye to everyone and everything you know? Describe the process from beginning to end. Was it all worth it? Why or why not?

965. There have been many horrible conflicts in the history of the world in which people have been forced out of their homes. Write a story in which you can only take the items you can carry and you must leave your house and most of your stuff behind. What or who has forced you to leave your home? Where would you go and what would you do next?

966. One of the most exciting parts of moving to a new place is discovering all the fun social activities that you can do there. What are the types of things and places you look for first when you move? What are the most exciting first discoveries you've made in your moves and why were they so special to you?

967. Moving can often signify a major event in one's life, such as going away to college, buying a house with a partner or getting a job in a new town. What was your most impacting move related to a major life event? How did your life change after that move?

968. After striking it rich, you and your family have literally moved into a castle. It seems your dad had secretly descended from royalty and now you're all part of a major royal family! How will you adjust after a move away from your friends and hometown right into the lap of luxury?

969. Before you and your family patch up the old house in the process of selling it, you decide to go around with a camera to document all of the marks you left behind. You see a record of you and your siblings' heights along with more than a few dings you left with a soccer ball. What are some of the other pieces of evidence in this house that you lived an exciting life in what will soon be your old home?

970. Imagine a future in which moving is literally a matter of coordinating a flight of your house, equipped with rocket boosters, from one location to another. You never actually need to leave the house at all

and can even sleep as your domicile moves from New York to Los Angeles in less than an hour. How would this newfangled technology change the world? Would it cause people to move more often or less often and why?

Questions

971. What is the first important question you ask someone when you're getting to know them? What does this particular question say about you?

972. Children are notorious for asking a lot of questions. Why do you think that is? Did you embody that stereotype as a child? Why or why not?

973. What is a question that you would never answer, no matter how close the person was asking it? What are the reasons you would never answer such a question?

974. After a long trip up a treacherous mountain, you have come upon an oracle who will answer three questions about anything at all. What questions do you ask? Are the answers what you were hoping for? Why or why not?

975. Have you ever asked a question you wish you hadn't? If so, what was the question and what were the consequences? If not, make up a situation in which you got more than you bargained for from what seemed like a simple question.

976. You have been appointed as Earth's first ambassador to an alien race! You may ask the alien high council one question. What do you ask, how do the aliens respond, and are you surprised to learn the answer?

977. Name a question that you love answering. What are some situations in which you'd like to be asked that question and why?

978. What is the question that best defines your internal struggle to understand life? Do you think you'll ever be able to answer that question? Why or why not?

979. As the top detective in your division, you have the first crack at a murder suspect in the interrogation room. What questions might you ask to get the information you need? Do you think the suspect is guilty? Why or why not?

980. If you could ask a family member any question, what would it be and why? Do you think they would answer it? Why or why not?

News

981. What do you think the amount of news you watch or read says about you? Would you say the amount of news you take in makes you an informed citizen? Why or why not?

982. How do you think news has changed in the last 30 years? Has it changed for better or worse and why?

983. How do you get most of your news? Do you think the different kinds of news affect the type of news we're exposed to? Why or why not?

984. You are a highly trusted journalist with your own show on a cable news network. What kind of news would you focus on broadcasting and why?

985. What kinds of news stories are most people interested in today? How does this news reflect what we care about as a society?

986. In 500 years, how do you think the nature of the news will have changed? Will people be more or less informed and why?

987. You wake up to find your picture on every news channel and blog in existence. What happened to make you so famous or infamous? What happens next?

988. What's the most captivating news story you've ever heard? What made it so interesting to you? Was it interesting to other people too? Why or why not?

989. Many people believe that most news stations are politically biased. Do you think a truly unbiased news station is possible? How would such a station keep from being biased?

990. If a journalist were to interview you about your life, what would be the most newsworthy aspect of your story? What kind of newsworthy things do you want to do in your lifetime and why?

Words

991. What do you think a person's everyday vocabulary says about them? What do you think your everyday vocabulary says about you and why?

992. Imagine that you needed to tell a friend something really important, but you just couldn't figure out the right words. What are some reasons you might have trouble? How would you get around this issue?

993. What word with more than five letters do you think you use the most? Why do you think that's your go-to word?

994. Think back to a time that you were really moved by a story, poem, or book. What was it about the words that made you feel different? Do you think you could ever create something like that? Why or why not?

995. What are five words that would gross you out if you heard them out loud? Which of them is the worst and why?

996. You've been teleported into the midst of an advanced society that does not use words. How do these beings communicate? How are you able to get them to understand you non-verbally?

997. They say that a picture is worth 1,000 words. What do you think that means? Do you agree? Why or why not?

998. You are the main sponsor of a bill that you're trying to get passed

in the U.S. Congress. How do you come up with the right words to convince your peers to vote for the bill? Are you successful? Why or why not?

999. What are some phrases your friends or family members use all the time? Do you think people in other parts of the country would understand those phrases? Why or why not?

1000. Do you think words are always enough when you're trying to make somebody understand your point of view? Why or why not?

INDEX

ABOUT THE AUTHORS

Bryan Cohen is an author, a creativity coach and an actor. Cohen is the author of creativity tools (*1,000 Creative Writing Prompts: Ideas for Blogs, Scripts, Stories and More*), self-help (*The Post-College Guide to Happiness*), fiction (*Ted Saves the World*) and thousands of blog posts around the web. He has published over 30 books, which have sold more than 20,000 copies in total. His website, BuildCreativeWritingIdeas.com, helps over 25,000 people a month to defeat writers block. In September, Cohen taped an episode for the nationally televised show, "Who Wants To Be A Millionaire." He lives with his wife in Chicago.

Jeremiah Jones is a comedian, an essayist and now an author. Jones recently graduated from the University of Clemson with a degree in English with an emphasis in writing and publication studies. He was a member of the university's long- and short-form improv troupe Mock Turtle Soup and was involved with many theatrical productions. Jones has published articles in the Easley Progress and the Pickens Sentinel. He currently lives in Chicago.

Made in the USA
Coppell, TX
13 February 2021

50294761R00059